Love and Anger

Good Relationships are on a Collision Course

Maurice Rapkin, PhD.
Eleanor Kendall

ISBN-13:
978-1508914020

ISBN-10:
1508914028

Contents

Love and Anger..3

Preface.. 1

How it Began January 1994 3

Journal First Lunch with Kay 17

Journal Groundhog Day 19

Journal Making of a Love Story 21

Journal Phone Conversation after 1^sty Lunch with Kay 23

Journal Second Lunch with Kay (About Session 1) 25

Session #2 Bad Dreams about Sam and Charlie 27

Journal After Session #2 Sam Meets Kay and Nick 29

Journal Session #3 How Sam and Molly Met.............................. 31

Session #3 Holly Reads Journal to Dr. Holman – The Critics...... 33

Journal #1 After Session #3 37

Journal #2 After Session #3 What Do I Want?.......................... 39

Session #4 Invisible Judges/Sun Bathing 41

Session #5 Stallion Dream – Passion and Punishment 45

Journal After Session #5 Mexican Dinner 47

Session #6 Critics and Pleasure 49

Journal 1 After Session #6 Sexual Fears........................ 51

Journal 2 After Session #6 Mammoth Mountain 53

Session #7 1st PAR with Sam: Co-fusion of Love/Anger 57

Journal #1 After Session #7 65

Journal #2 After Session #7 Dinner for Eight – Inner/Outer World.............. 67

Session #8 Dome with Charlie.. 69

Journal #1 After Session #8 73

Journal #2 After Session #8 75

Journal Before Session #9 Tuesday Evening 77

Session #9 Two Vows – Wednesday Evening........................ 79

Journal #1 After Session #9 Wednesday Night 83

Journal #2 After Session #9 Thursday Morning 85

Journal Before Session #10 87

Session #10 89

Journal #1 after Session #10 1st Two-chair Dialogue 91

Journal #2 after Session #10 2nd Two-chair Dialogue 93

In Place of Session #11 Journal #1 Molly Tells Same about Alcoholic Parents 95

In Place of Session #11 Journal #2 Mom, Sam, Molly Journal ... 97

In Place of Session #11 Journal #3 Sam and Mom Can Meet 99

Journal #1 in Place of Session #12 Mother Goes to Hospital 101

Journal #2 in Place of Session #12 After I Took Mom to the Hospital 103

Journal #3 in Place of Session #12 Diagnosis and Prognosis 105

Journal #4 in Place of Session #12 Molly's Jealousies 107

Journal #5 Session #12 Swimming Pool – Fantasy with Andy ... 109

Journal #6 Session #12 Topanga Beach with Andy 111

Journal #7 Session #12 Conversation with Kay re: Andy and Sam 113

Session #13 Journal #1 Hospital / Molly and Andy go out for an Ice Cream Cone 115

Session #13 Journal #2 Molly Asks Sam to Wait 117

Session #13 Journal #3 Sara Feels Left Out (re: Andy) 119

Session #13 Journal #4 Chasing the Blues Away 121

Session #13 Journal #5 Forgiveness 123

Session #13 Journal #6 The Day Mom Dies 125

Session #13 Journal #7 Molly & Andy Talk to Sara 127

Session #13 Journal #8 Molly Comforts Andy 129

Session #13 Journal #9 Sara's Eulogy 131

Session #13 Sam at the Funeral at the Back of the Church 133

Session #13 Session after Mother's Death 135

Journal #1 Before Session #14 Andy's Kisses Defy Death 137

Journal #2 Before Session #14 After the Funeral 139

Session #14 Andy and Molly with Holman 1st Session Joint Therapy Session 141

Journal #1 After Session #14 Healing Anger with Andy............ 145

Journal #1 Before Session #15 Bathtub Fantasy......................... 147

Session #15 I Love Two Men 149

Journal #1 after Session #15 Dilemma of Being in Love with 2 Men............ 153

Journal #2 after Session #15 Still I love Myself......................... 155

Journal #1 Before Session #16 Sara's Blow Up II...................... 157

Session #16 Molly and Andy with Dr. Holman......................... 159

Journal #1 after Session #16 No More Blaming Me or Andy 165

Journal #2 after Session #16 At the Restaurant 167

Session #17 Gem Dream.. 169

Journal #1 after Session #17 How Clever the Unconscious Is ... 171

Journal #2 after Session #17 Loving Feelings 173

Journal Instead of Session #18 Dialogue with my Dead Mother 175

Journal #1 Before Session #19 Before Cabo 179

Journal #2 Before Session #19 Arrival in Cabo........................ 181

Journal #3 Before Session #19 What We Like About Each Other 183

Journal #4 Before Session #19 Spin the Bottle.......................... 187

Journal #5 Before Session #19 Love and Lust............................ 189

Journal #6 Before Session #19 Intimacy.................................... 191

Session #19 After Cabo 193

Journal Before Session #20 Taking Andy to the Airport........... 195

Session #20 Loss After Andy Leaves in Holman's Office 197

Session #21 The Victim Returns... 199

Journal #1 instead of Session #22 Going to Malibu 201

Journal #2 instead of Session #22 3AM in Malibu.................... 205

Journal #1 instead of Session #23 Driving Home from Malibu .209

Epilogue 213

Author Bio Eleanor Kendall 215

Author Bio Maurice Rapkin.. 217

Anger As A Hot Potato: Constructive Options in Handling Anger.. 219

Pretending, Thinking and Feeling in Psychotherapy 231

IS "JUSTIFIED ANGER" AN EVASION OF REALITY 243

P A R — PRETEND ANGER RELEASE 253

Gems...256

Acknowledgement

This book could (would) not have possibly been written without the collaboration of a dedicated group of writers working to create this book about love and anger.

This group of writers was organized by Eleanor Kendall.

The writers were Maurice Rapkin, Ph.D., Eleanor Kendall, Gail O'Neill, and Gaylord Burke Littenberg as a story consultant and collaborating with Dr. Rapkin.

The book celebrates the contribution of Dr. Rapkin who spent 50 years of his professional life creating and developing a definitive concept of anger as expressed in his published pamphlet titled "Anger is a Hot Potato".

Other important contributions with years of involvement were Gail O'Neill, Ph.D., who wrote, rewrote, edited and kept 6 boxes of organized files. Michelle Lathan was the brilliant typist and computer expert. Eleanor Kendall has had a 50 year professional relation with Dr. Rapkin, first as a therapy client and later as a gifted counselor in her own right, supervised by Dr. Rapkin.

Eleanor Kendall's husband, Lee Kendall, has over the years held the book together and ultimately is responsible for having the book, "Love and Anger", published. Lee always believed in the book!

FOREWORD

Ten years before I wrote Men Are From Mars, Women Are From Venus, one of my most significant mentors was the clinical psychologist, Maurice Rapkin. He was a part of the first wave of psychologists to provide new insights for successfully applying psychology in private practice. Maurice was a pioneer in the early days of client centered research and as a result, fifty years later, his ideas regarding Love and Anger permeate most modern approaches to improve communication in all relationships.

Maurice was a giant in his field and provided a basis for the many ideas that I have also promoted in my many books. One of his major themes was that anger, either expressed, unexpressed or suppressed, is a major block to increasing intimacy and improved communication. Through fully understanding this powerful emotion he revealed how one could most effectively restore feelings of love, trust and affection.

Rather than seek to avoid or suppress anger or even shout it out as so many of his contemporaries were suggesting, he discovered the keys to transform anger into love. He explained that all anger arises from blocked positive impulse wishes. Through a variety of approaches anyone could learn how to transform anger back into love.

Those who could receive his insight in therapy were truly blessed with a new ability to lower stress in their lives and insure a lifetime of love. Although Maurice has passed on, his message lives on in this story about Love and Anger. I trust that you too will benefit from his wisdom as it is expressed in real life drama, with characters acting out their journey of applying his many insights for increasing happiness and fulfillment.

John Gray, Author of Men Are From Mars, Women Are From Venus

Preface

Someone said that when you write down a story, you live it all over again. By writing it down and reading it, you feel empowered to feel and to re-experience the excitement, discovery and desire.

Chapter 1 of my love story is a time everyone in Los Angeles will remember. I prefer it as the night my orgasmic explosion rocked the earth.

How it Began
January 1994

I was eating and drinking again, smoking the occasional Camel when I met Sam at a Christmas party in Malibu. The biannual diet was over, the move into Spirit was fading, and the hunt for a mate had begun. From the start, sensuous kisses were our medium and our message. It translated as more, more, more. Our chief mode of communication was the kiss, the underestimated kiss, the unsung heart and soul of sex and love. We'd kiss in between sips of wine, in between bits of brie, wet kisses, kisses in the middle of sentences, our mouths full, longing, hungry mouths, kissing everywhere, but especially in restaurants waiting for our meal to be served. We had our own personal version of the cocktail hour, our own "hors d'ouevres" as Sam used to call them, kissing complements to the fine cheeses and Melba toast, to the penne drenched in olive oil.

I don't remember much talking in those early days, not a relevant word of interest or insight. But the talk didn't matter. It was the kissing that mattered. And the eating and the drinking. We ordered icy vodka martinis up, extra dry, two olives, two onions. We toasted ourselves grandly, saluting our courageous pursuit of feeling, all while numbing all feeling.

With Sam, I always wanted more. I felt it in my throat, in my stomach, a longing as palpable as starvation, and as deadly. I wanted to consume everything in sight, including him. It wasn't so much that I wanted to have sex with him as I wanted to eat him up, and not just in small, kiss-sized bites either. I wanted to devour big chunks of him, an upper arm, a broad shoulder, his neck, his chest, that perfectly plump belly. I wanted to eat him up, the way I eat rare roast beef, preferably the outside cut, or baked potatoes with sour cream and chives—in gulps, pushing pieces of him in so fast that not a minute went by that I wasn't tasting his salt, his sweet, his spice. If I didn't eat him quickly, I might lose my sense of taste or he might disappear, or some Big Person might come along and clear my plate before I was finished.

I was addicted. Sam's hobby is cooking, gourmet cooking, and my pleasure is eating. What a striking match! Eating and kissing with Sam whet my appetite for more, for more food faster, for one drink drunker. He became symbolic of youth and freedom and beauty. And all of it, dressed up as a Caesar Salad, Linguini Alfredo and a fine Merlot.

Like all serious drinkers, I wanted the perfect drink to complement the day, the hour, the meal. Sunday brunch meant gin fizzes. Saturday morning called for bloody mary's with curly sticks of celery to stir the ice and chill the mind. Friday night demanded shots of Patron, and Monday nights, the weekend over, white wine in summer, red wine in winter. Sam became synonymous with all the foods I loved as a child, foods that comforted and soothed. He became my homemade special: peanut butter and honey on toast, sweet warmth dripping down and around the edges. He became the world's best hamburger, the "Hickory Cheese" from the Apple Pan on Pico Boulevard in Los Angeles. He became the finest cheese enchilada I ever tasted from the first Mexican restaurant ever to grace the Westside. Sam knew almost as quickly as I that he had found his compadre, his hedonistic soul mate. He had finally met the starving woman of his dreams. Lucky Sam. But I, too was dying of thirst. And so his courtship consisted of temptation: he lured me everywhere with kisses and cooking, flirting mercilessly with my life-long hunger, inviting bad habits back. Somehow, he managed to keep satisfaction at a distance; instead, he inspired insatiability. I couldn't get enough. I had always wanted more, needed more; there just wasn't enough. And with Sam it was okay to want more and to take in more, more peanut butter, more bread and honey, more of his heat, his tender touch, more sugar, caramelized, convincing. There *is* paradise on earth and I had just landed. Boom! I was in the lush thickness of it, in the loving arms of one Samuel S. Brennan.

In January 1994, I sat cooing on my kitchen stool, Sam standing between my knees, sneaking kisses. It was early in our relationship and we hadn't had much "intimate" time together. All we'd managed to do was "meet in the middle" to eat and drink. In fact, we'd just gotten home from Kabu Japanese restaurant and Kirin beers.

My twelve-year-old daughter, Sara, was in her room, stereo blasting. I felt we were fairly safe as long as the Beastie Boys or Indigo Girls were blaring, but as our kisses grew in intensity, I knew we had to get away. I wanted to be young and in love. We had to go somewhere, anywhere. This thing had to be consummated. We had to get out from beneath Sara's newly-acquired parental scrutiny. She had been doing a lot of strict mothering since I'd met Sam. She sensed I was different: a return to adolescence, about thirty years' worth of regression. And, inasmuch as I had found the perfect Peter Pan partner, I had to sneak away from my daughter, this new "mom."

Sam was my new "boyfriend." He was like my prey, my find, a delicious piece of filet mignon. I needed to get out from under Sara's critical eye so I could eat him up in peace. I had to find a way out of the confines of my role as mother and model citizen. I wanted darkness and privacy. It was time to devour my kill. But where? Where do middle-aged parents-turned-lovers go? Where could we get down to some serious mutual consumption of one another?

It was a Sunday night, and the following Monday was Martin Luther King's birthday and a school holiday. Susan, our neighbor next door and Sara's best friend, had spent the entire weekend at our house. Their plans for the evening were still in negotiation but *nothing* was developing. Perhaps it was Sara's wariness of Sam, I don't know. It seemed she didn't want to leave us alone. I felt awkward and guilty about even wanting to leave them. I tried to push Plan A, which was a sleep-over at Susan's. And at that point, I would have liked it if Sara moved out for a week!

Of course, she sensed this. She may not have known it on a conscious level, but she needed to throw a wrench into my leaving, certainly into my new relationship, maybe into my life. Or it felt that way. She dragged her puppy-large feet, she whined, "Hey Mom, maybe we don't *want* to go to Susan's house," or "I don't know what we're going to do. Why's it so important?"

I'm not the kind of parent that dictates. Sometimes I wish I could. But as I looked at frustrated Sam, I knew I had to do something. I didn't wait around to see what plans panned out. I didn't engage in arguing. I didn't play "rug" or "dog." In a burst of decision, I grabbed Sam's hand and walked out the front door with a casual, "We'll see you guys later," over my left shoulder, careful not to make eye contact. I said

I would call to see if they had landed a satisfying plan. If not, I foolishly added, I would return.

So, into the cool January night the young lovers fled, both of us in our forties, casting our fate to the winds. Off we went, cruising like kids right next to each other in Sam's red and white '59 Chevy convertible, affectionately called Bessie. With windows down, Eric Clapton's "Layla" serenading the neighborhood, Sam's right hand found its way up my skirt. We were "Spin and Marty," lots of energy. But nowhere to put it, no place to go.

Spin: So, where should we go, Marty?
Marty: I don't know, Spin, where do you think we should go?
Spin: I don't know, you choose. You're the boy.
Marty: If it were up to me, we'd pull over under that tree and I'd have you right now.
Spin: Hey...I know a place...A romantic inn tucked away in Malibu. You can hear the surf *plus,* they've got a bar and restaurant.
Marty: I don't know, that sounds far away and pricey.

With that last line, Sam's hand, hiking half way up my thigh, wasn't nearly as exciting. He'd introduced reality. Before our destination could be reached, I needed a drink. And I needed food. Feeling a bit let down, I became coy. I pushed his hand away from The Prize, suggesting we slow down and think. We drove around, not knowing where in the world young lovers go.

He turned off at Pico onto the Avenue of the Stars. There were no private places where we could just be alone – only shops and high rises. We passed the new Lunamare Hotel. It was on the other side of a grassy center divider. When I suggested we go there, Sam winced. I felt another twinge of reality. Maybe money was an issue ...

The hotel was brand new, a sparkling jewel of a place, lights twinkling, inviting lovers from around the world to seduce and be seduced. It called out our names and here we were! Ready, set, go: two kids who can eat and drink and kiss all day and into the night because there is no sense of time and there are no consequences.

"Do you really want to go to this kind of a glitzy place?" A little voice inside my head began to chant "yes" to the elegant new hotel. It was close to home, it was new and it was all swanked out; it was   just what the doctor ordered. Besides, hotels are always romantic, sexy places to be. It had to have a bar, had to have a dining room, had to have lots of beautiful bedrooms, maybe even a wedding suite. It was perfectly expensive and perfectly inexpensive: it wasn't the Ritz Carlton, or the Four Seasons, but it wasn't the Motel 6 either. My mind was made up, though I sensed Sam's lack of enthusiasm.

I deserve it, I thought. I put my hand on *his* thigh making it talk to him as I said, "I love sheets with 500 thread count, down pillows and blackout curtains. I want to tuck you in and kiss you goodnight with champagne bubbles tickling my tongue and with juicy strawberries in my mouth."

"Okay." And then a bigger "*Okay.*" I felt his readiness.

Sam is no fool. He knows which way a woman's wind blows, and he didn't want to blow his chance by arguing with me. What he guessed, to put it delicately, was that he was about to get laid. And if we went to the Lunamare, he was right. Sam also knows that hotels are fertile ground for spending money and, I found out later, he didn't have any. "Not this year, anyway," he said. "Used to, though. Used to pop into the Four Seasons as a matter of fact, have a few drinks, get a suite, jacuzzi, the works." Swell, I thought. Thanks for sharing.

In a second, he made a misguided left, up and over the curb, his old Chevy wearily groaning in resignation. "Here he goes again," I could hear old Bessie say. So up and across the newly planted landscaping she climbed, Sam grinning, being adorably young and reckless. I played Natalie Wood to his James Dean, saying, "Oh, no, Sam, don't! You'll wreck the flowers!" All sense left me as I watched his rugged good looks, his adept handling of old Bessie, his openness to me and to love. I couldn't contain my giggling. I loved it, I loved him, I loved our future, I loved my antique-white wedding dress, the chapel in Santa Barbara, the honeymoon in Italy. And I believed in love, sweet love, really being "lovelier the second time around." This was it. Again, again, and again, this was *IT*!

A handsome uniformed doorman opened Sam's door. "Good evening, sir. Welcome to the new Lunamare."

We walked into the lobby feeling young. Old jeans, no luggage, disheveled, without a care in the world. There was no other moment but Right Now. And because of our youth, we owned the joint. Alas, there was the bar, brand new, waiting for us, as bars always are, a gracious host offering peanuts and pretzels, a cocktail or two, home, Mom, love – all of it, waiting there just for us.

After two martinis each, another element of the bar scene reared its sexy head: lowered inhibition and an increased sex drive. The hunger for "fusion" with Sam, the wanting to climb in, on, or beneath him, the wanting to get closer, closer to feast on connection and acceptance there, the need to find peace in him or at least with him, we longed for that strange peace and freedom that comes from an insatiable craving. With each sip of vodka, each nibble of one of the six Spanish olives in my martini, the so-called "drive" that my ex-husband said I didn't have, surprised even me. I couldn't keep my hands off Sam, touching him in places and in ways I was taught in Catholic schools never to do. "It tempts the boys, teases them unfairly," the nuns told us. And, of course, all *that* was the work of the "devil." We were taught to avoid the "near occasion of sin" at all costs. Naturally, it was the near occasion of sin, the closeness to danger that excited me most.

All of a sudden, a motherly thought intruded. I jumped up, excused myself, and went to the ladies room to call Sara. She had finally decided she was going to Susie's. Okay, the stage was set. The coast was clear. The fruit was ripe for the picking. I strutted back to the bar, turning heads all the while. One kiss later, we were sashaying toward the front desk.

We were shown to a suite overlooking Fox Studios. I'm not sure at that point what I found sexier; the luxury of the room on top of the world or my sweet sloshed Sam, my future husband, the answer to my prayers.

I marched across the lengthy living room, a woman with a mission. Picking up the phone with authority as well as breeding, I called ever-loving room service to see if they had Some More Food. With a wink to Sam, I ordered him cornbread and fried chicken, and a tall orange juice (which we planned on filling with the vodka that was in the no-host bar of our refrigerator). For myself, I ordered mashed potatoes and gravy, a side of broccoli, and their famous chocolate mousse pie. When I hung up, Sam was behind me with one of my breasts in each hand. I giggled girlishly. I pushed him away and gleefully addressed the broad selection of food and drinks under lock and key in the mini-bar. I opened a beer for myself and a tiny Smirnoff for Sam. But he wasn't so interested in his drink. He was thinking about sex. I was thinking about food, and how I was in charge, and rich and young and free. Life was so full of possibility, and best of all, there were no responsibilities. I owed no one anything. I wasn't obliged to anyone. I didn't have to take care of anyone but me. And to my knowledge, the best way to do that was to eat. At least to eat first. And to drink.

Sam had his clothes off in a nano-second, and was waiting between the cool sheets of a California King for me to shed my many layers, my protective skins. I dallied. There were curtains to close, French doors to open, then close, testing the amount of light they would let in. There was the radio to turn on, candles to search for, a Bible to find, the television to turn off, the bathroom to visit—on and on, I dallied.

When I finally climbed into bed, fully clothed, Sam had begun to drift off. I played with his hair, I flirted, diverted and distracted. It worked for awhile, until he became impatient. "Jesus, what's with all these clothes?" We began to kiss and kiss some more, while he struggled to undress me. I didn't help at all. In fact, I got in his way as much as I could.

Finally, there was no way out. It was time for the Dance of the Seven Veils. I allowed him to begin the process of unbuttoning my blouse in such a way as to preclude my being seen uncompromisingly or unbecomingly. He played along, but I noticed he was losing steam. The alcohol was pulling its reverse number. His sugar-high energy was being converted into a sugar-low downer. I sat up, seducing his mouth with kisses and at the same time diverting his attention to my face and away from my breasts. I pulled the little blouse up and over my head with a few added seconds of stretching my arms above my head to show off my small waist, a source of personal pride). I looked at Sam and he was flat-out gone. I was successful. Again, sex postponed. He had been leaning on his arm watching me until *boom!* he fell over.

It's amazing how men can all do that, I thought. They fall asleep like newborns. They can be here one syllable and gone the next. Well, this particular night it was fine by me. My dance could wait. Where was that damned room service? I'd called at least half an hour earlier.

I turned on the hottest water I could stand in the huge marble bathtub, using the entire bottle of bubble bath. Within seconds, I was smothered in bubbles. They were everywhere and they were doing for me what I couldn't do for myself, hiding my body.

Sexually, I'm a fraud. I've been told that I'm sexy, but frankly, sex terrifies and confuses me. There are only three things that really scare me: people, financial insecurity, and my own sexuality, or lack thereof. None of these fears show much because I'm great at covering up. Though not as wild as I want to *seem,* when it comes right down to the moment when I have to deliver the goods, that point when I have to strip or get stripped of my almost-professional cover, certain panic sets in.

It's at this juncture that I begin my now-famous dance, my strip tease, my attempt to trip and trick the lights fantastic. I call it my Dance of the Seven Veils. I am a magician: now you see me, now you don't. I'm masterful at sleight of hand and sleight of body. I know how to play dodge ball in bed. Fear of being seen, perhaps even scrutinized, terrifies me more than any thief or robber. I appear to be all chocolate, whipped cream and liqueur, level upon geologic level of whole grain alcohol and sugar. But when the plates have been cleared, and the coffee cups filled, it's time to serve La Piece de Resistance. That is when I begin my disappearing act. The fear of being "found out," of being seen, of it being discovered that I may be heavier than I appear in my clothes, more pendulously breasted than I seem, more thighed, more stretch-marked and blue veined than might be expected rules me.

All of this is a roller-coaster ride of terror inside my head. The fears line up, and what a strong frontline they are! They destroy all possibility of my having any real fun in bed. They preclude pleasure as sure as if they knifed it to death.

So when you get right down to it, I can't charge the night or the light fantastic at all. I'm a wimp, a failure, a fuck-up at fucking. How can anyone be a fuck-up at fucking? It's almost impossible to screw up even the so-called worst fuck. How bad can it be? But I can't trudge through that jungle naked. I can't tolerate being seen. I'm too scared of being judged.

It's most disconcerting to pretend that you want something as sexy as sex only to find that you aren't pretending. I really do want it. Or rather, I want to want it. I want to like it when I get it. I want to relax my mind and body so I can feel what is touching me and feel what I'm touching. I want sexual feelings to match feelings of love and affection.

I turned the radio to almost full-blast, an "oldies but goodies" station. Once in the jacuzzi, I got a brilliant idea. Jacuzzi jet streams, I remembered my friend telling me, mean quick orgasms; and if you tease yourself with the water a little, great ones. Making love to myself in Sam's stead, with Sam in the next room, added a touch of naughtiness. It was glorious, a symphony of iridescence, an explosion of fantasies. Maybe he would wake up and quietly steal toward the bathroom door. Maybe he was *watching* me. Such thoughts both thrilled and terrified me. It was perfect. The alcohol had energized me and the hot water relaxed me. I bounced high and low, bubbles bubbling, water both soothing and exciting, as I reveled in my fantasies in the bath.

The knock at our door sent me splashing to regain consciousness and composure. I grabbed one of the luxurious hotel bathrobes, threw a towel around my wet head, and coolly answered the door. "Room service," a man's voice announced. Oh, yes, room service. I opened the door to a flat-faced, too-old-to-be-up-this-late gentleman who wheeled in an elaborately set cart, complete with faux silver and a gold-toothed smile. He waited. I stood there stupidly. We looked at each other dumbly. Then I got it, a tip. I scrounged around in my purse. Nothing there as usual. I yanked Sam's jeans from the floor and flung a five at him, all I could find. "Good night, Ma'am," he chirped. "Enjoy your stay at the Lunamare." This last bit he added as a post-script, halfway out the door, as though he hadn't even noticed it was two o'clock in the morning and he'd just delivered two meals to one woman who was dripping wet and drunk.

Sam did not stir. I had imagined that my signing "Mrs. Samuel Brennan" so broadly might have awakened him. I smirked to myself, in fact, envisioning Sam, stark-ass naked, bolting out of the bedroom after sensing my silent claim to all his worldly goods (or what was left of them after his divorce). But no such pleasure was to be mine. He snored on, ever the innocent.

I wanted to *eat* more than I wanted to finish what I had started in the bathtub so I left the bubbles behind, maybe to be used later when Sam could join me. Now, I thought, *this* is what I call fun. I turned on the television, something that doesn't come naturally to me, dropping the wet towel on the floor. I wanted to play dress-up.

Painstakingly, piece by lovely smelling piece, I put on Sam's clothes. First. his old faded and frayed jeans without his or my underwear; then his white oxford button-down shirt that smelled surprisingly of Atkinson's Royal Briar, I was sure of it. That was my father's after-shave. I used to love to smell anything my father had touched because it had that rich masculine scent, plus cigarettes, plus alcohol. I stood there in the middle of the living room, rocking myself gently, smelling Sam and Daddy and me, all three of us there in that shirt. After a minute, I dropped to the floor to put on Sam's new, white cotton socks. Rising shakily, I "rock n rolled" over to the mirror feeling pretty and cool. I wished Sam could see me. He would fall in love for sure if he weren't there already.

The only thing on the television was some talk show, the name of which escapes me. I pulled the dinner cart over in front of me, pulled up a Victorian chair, and began to delicately devour both our dinners. I was dressed in his clothes, eating his food. I felt omnipotent and independent like one of the Georges, Eliot or Sand, either one would do. I struck various poses to see which one best suited my fantasy: one leg up on the chair, one down, thoughtfully, like Jo in *Little Women*; or both legs apart, the way men sit.

As a little girl, I was hypnotized by the way men sat, legs akimbo, open, displaying themselves like dogs in the sun, their pants and egos bulging. They were so unselfconscious. And looking back on it, their taking up so much space was arrogant. I envied them their freedom of movement, even as a child. I remembered trying to steal my eyes away and I remembered how they, or rather their groins, fascinated me as I tried not to look. But this night, with Sam, the memories of my father's friends excited me anew. I wasn't a little girl anymore and there was a living, breathing dream-man sprawled less than five feet away. And, the best news, he was mine for the asking.

Sam was asleep and temporarily unavailable; there was food in front of me, food that needed eating. My forty-ish and aching back started to bother me (I needed more alcohol), so I ditched all thoughts of waking up Sam for some "sweet lovin." Instead, I chose the Indian or Yogi style of sitting on the plush carpet, feet tucked beneath me like a teenager: lean, supple, pre-sexual and feasting. In the back of my mind, posed thus, I briefly hoped again that Sam would awaken. If only he could find me there, sensual and sexy in his clothes, deliciously greasy-mouthed from gnawing on his cornbread fried chicken. I wanted him to walk in, himself naked and edible, lusting after me lusting after the next bit of his next course. Or better, I envisioned him watching me from the bedroom, peering through the French doors so lightly curtained in pale organza, perfect for the voyeur I hoped he was, so perfect for creating illusion, mystery and an erection.

"He is worthless," I thought, suddenly angry at him for being such a damn drunk. I mumbled as much aloud, flung open the French doors, and stomped over to the bed. At least he was still breathing. I made enough noise to awaken even a heavy sleeper, but the booze had done its job. He was passed-ass-out.

After the late, late show, I called it quits. It was after 3 o'clock in the morning, but the hour was no match for the alcohol, which has always had the opposite effect on me than it had on Sam. It not only keeps me up, I can feel the blood traveling through my veins. My heart's beat is strong enough to hear across the room. My legs get excited with the childhood cramps my mother called "growing pains." I am ready to run and play.

Sam's clothes are already off, so I climbed in beside him purposely clumsily. I reached over and kissed his neck. I lay still, breathing and listening to the microphone my heart had become through the speakers my ears had become. I coughed. Nothing worked. None of it worked to awaken my young Irish lad. So I went for the jugular: I lit a cigarette. It only took a minute of the smoke filtering past his red nose. He rose up on one elbow, suddenly not groggy in the least, and grabbed the cigarette out of my hand. He reached over my nakedness to put it out, stabbing at the ashtray with authority. He discovered my breast along the way back, and we were off and running. We began our love-making as though we'd never stopped. Rocking and rolling, kissing, devouring. He said I smelled delicious, a strange combination of gardenia and garlic. It was as though he hadn't been asleep for three hours, as though I hadn't eaten two dinners, watched late-night television, as though I hadn't played Splendor in the Grass in the bath tub with fine oils and endless bubbles, washed my hair or played dress-up in his clothes. It was kisses again, intense and passionate as our first starving kisses hours earlier that afternoon when we ate Japanese food with chopsticks, feeding one another sukiyaki and popcorn shrimp, guzzling Kirin beer.

Sam was very good at foreplay. In fact, he prided himself on how fine his foreplay was. He said, "It's all in the hors d'oeuvres, Molly, my little dumpling. The hors d'oeuvres are better than the main course!" And his appetizers were incroyables. Corn-nibbled ears, suckling-sweet toes, lightly-bitten nipples, slightly-pulled hair, then, the coup de gras, a lovely light swat on the fanny. I was being feasted upon, and slowly. I was his banquet, and believe it, Sam takes his meals seriously. He doesn't just eat dinner like the rest of us. He dines. So after more appetizers than most women dare to wish for, he slid onto and into me all in one smooth move.

We were drunk but alert and loose. We were paying attention. It felt like the first-time-ever. "A slow fuck," he whispered in my ear. "A slow fuck," I repeated. "I like that, a slow fuck." I not only liked the sound of it, but its meaning began to sink in, with each repetition. The physical reinforcement of this particular translation of "slow" drove me deeper and deeper into hypnosis, into his definition of "slow" and his definition of "fuck."

"That's right," he encouraged. "Yes, go real slow now," he said. "Slower...slower than even that." The words crawled out of his mouth, fat morsels of sound, juicy and dirty and inspiring.

And then, subtly, slowly, the slow fuck began to get just a little faster. We gathered speed slowly, then faster still. I began to feel more and more height. The gear shifted. The momentum changed. The world was turning, the earth, the wondrous earth was moving, just like I'd heard it would.

I knew this was more than the most profound love-making, more than the most explosive orgasm.

The room was moving, we were sliding from side to side in it. The furniture was moving. This was more, much more than I had ever, ever imagined.

I could hear the still-filled Jacuzzi sloshing back and forth, a small sea in a storm. Water slapping the sides making sounds of Victory at Sea. I looked over Sam's shoulder and saw the water come up and over, onto the marble floor. Was it moving or was it me? Us?

The television moved out of its huge cupboard. Tiny bottles of liquor spilled out of the opened refrigerator door ringing like bells against each other. The plates, cups and bowls soared off the dinner cart, lamps flew off tables. Combs, keys, money, cigarettes, glasses, bottles, purses, soaps, shampoo, conditioner, condoms all went flying. Sam, who had slipped out and away from me for a second, came to, and realized this wasn't the earthquake he was used to creating during sex --- we were having an EARTHQUAKE, a living monster of an earthquake. Sam flung himself over me as I repeated in barely audible animal tones, "My child, my child, my child, my child..." The words that might have been added, the conventions of language that might have made those two words into sentences were not forthcoming. We were going to die. The ninth floor of the fancy new Lunamare was going to explode, burst into flames, break off from itself, and crash to the ground. I was going to die. And what in God's name, was happening to my child?

The lights, all electricity went out everywhere. The motion stopped. It took hours to stop, days, lifetimes. But it finally did. I jumped up fast, and foolishly grabbed the phone. No. I tried to turn on a light. No. I searched the drawers for a flashlight. No. Then out of a nightmare of wild images and fog, Sam snapped, "Let's get out of here. Get dressed." I sort of came to. He picked up a lamp and tried to turn it on. No, no, no, nothing worked. We found our clothes: They were soaking wet so we searched for our hotel bathrobes, stumbling, bumping into furniture and each other, but nothing was funny. When Sam finally found the door, we saw others in their white robes, saw ghosts floating down the hall, grim-faced, silent, scared. We followed them. A man with a flashlight in a uniform was leading the way down the stairs. We all held hands, all struck dumb, some half-drunk, half asleep, all wondering if maybe we were already dead and this was "but a dream." We followed the leader like lambs. Finally, nine flights of stairs later, we were at the bottom and out of the god-forsaken building. We were safe, we were alive. An amazing concept on the heels of maybe-dead. We stood on a grassy knoll, in the middle of the Avenue of the Stars, with strangers, people from all over the world. Visitors to lovely Los Angeles, to sunny Southern California. I couldn't laugh and I couldn't cry. It was much bigger than laughter, far bigger than tears.

We united, huddling close against each other, against the unknown and the cold, in complete darkness, in front of the magnificent sets of Twentieth Century Fox, where myths are created, where pretend is made real, where make-believe was born. Not a syllable was uttered by anyone. We were alive. We were silent and we were one.

Within seconds, I "came to" for a second time, or was it the third, the fourth? I whispered to Sam that we had to get the car out from valet parking. He knew what I was thinking: Sara. Without a word, he walked soberly (and I think now almost stately) toward the doorman whose official green gabardine jacket with braided epaulets of gold gave him an air of authority. God, how I loved Sam at that moment, taking charge, taking care of business, taking care of me, taking care of Sara.

My heart stopped when he returned to me saying that there was no way anyone, with the emphasis on anyone, could access a car parked at the hotel. I grabbed his hand and started walking.

His gait quickly outpaced mine and he pulled me along. No matter how fast, though, none of what we passed as we walked toward   home went unnoticed. I saw fallen trees, broken glass, water mains exploded. It looked like war on Pico Boulevard. Sara's school, the church, the restaurants we frequented, the park where she'd gone for puppy-training --- my mixed up head was already grieving and geared up for loss. A steady recitation of made-up prayers bumped into a steady recitation of fears and worries that collided with tears of gratitude just to be alive. But my being alive would only have meaning if Sara were alive too. Sam, as I might have predicted had I known him better or longer, was calm and steadfast and re-assuring. Squeezing my hand, his words were like a calming, pain reliever. He was my doctor, my leader, my priest, my friend.

He led me straight to the street where I live. Every neighbor we ever knew was sanding in the street. Everyone, that is, except me. Sara's eyes said "Where were you?" She was terrified. I was over come. I hugged away her questions until a later time when we could talk. That later time never came.

I was in awe, in shock, in fear and in love with Sam, no doubt about it. I was (and am still) grateful to the Gods that such a trick or twist of destiny should have brought me what I needed at the exact time I needed it. If there had to be an earthquake, I'm eternally grateful that the earthlings were able to produce a Sam and the stars decided to cross at that precise and perfect angle allowing us to meet, to fall, to be caught, and then amazingly, to be in each other's arms on January 17, 1994 at 4:04 in the morning.

Journal
First Lunch with Kay

A few weeks later I was sitting in the corner window of Lilly's, a small French restaurant in Brentwood, nursing my iced tea and waiting for my friend Kay. She has been my sage and confidante since the days when she was my teacher and I was a rebellious adolescent in Catholic school.

Madame Lilly cam over, kissed my cheeks, and asked if my friend was coming to meet me today.

The charming restaurant has lead-paned windows, dressed with French provincial stripes and prints in lush pink and paisley coordinating with the upholstered chairs and cushions. The highly waxed, well worn floors are a warm terracotta tile.

I felt exhilarated on this particular day. When the waiter appeared, I ordered two champagne cocktails. I felt like celebrating life and love with Kay.

Just then she arrived at the table, sparkling and happy to see me. "To love," I toasted, as she sat down and we clicked our flutes.

"Oh, Kay," I said, leaning toward her. "I'm in love and I think I want to *marry* this man." With that, we both gulped down half a glassful. The champagne and thoughts of love flushed our faces and we began to giggle.

"Tell me more," Kay invited.

"Well, Sam and I have seen each other nearly every day for six weeks. Sam's so sweet. He includes Sara in some of our time together, taking her with us for lunch or dinner. Sara really likes him. I can't wait for you and Nick to meet him."

Kay said, "I can't wait myself. Let's make a plan before we leave. Molly, I can already see the effect being in love with Sam is having on you." Kay got up and kissed my flushed cheek.

"I love you, Kay."

Kay told me she loved me too. We picked up our menus and started to read, but I couldn't focus. After a few moments, I whispered to Kay, "The truth is, I'm scared." After ordering, I continued. "Ever since the night of the earthquake, I've had trouble sleeping. Sometimes I'm awakened by bad dreams and I'm scared to go back to sleep.

"In my dreams, I feel like I'm losing someone, either Sara or my mother, and sometimes it's Sam. Once he was swimming toward me, but the tide carried him away. Why am I having these awful nightmares?

"It's odd. Here I am feeling so happy, and at the same time I'm feeling so fearful. I worry that I'm going to lose this relationship like I have the others. I don't understand what happens. I start relationships with such good intentions, and then something happens. You know, Kay, it's already been five years since Andy and I divorced." We were interrupted by the rich scents of our bouillabaisse and coquille St. Jacques.

Kay shook her head. "It's hard to believe."

Molly whispered, "I don't want to lose Sam! What can I do to make sure this lasts?"

Kay asked me, "What do you think about consulting a professional?"

After a moment, I asked if she knew anyone.

"I do. If I were you, I'd try Dr. Larry Holman. He's my psychologist, and he's very good with relationships. Nick and I attended his seminar on love and anger last summer. I thought he had helpful insights into what can go wrong; his belief is that anger is what bends relationships out of shape," Kay explained.

"It sounds like a good idea, Kay. I think I need help to have the kind of relationship I've always wanted to create."

Journal
Groundhog Day

Every morning I look out the window hoping to see the famous groundhog. It's been raining for days! I've made up a story. The day that silly groundhog comes out and stays out will signal the end of my pain. My fingers are crossed . . .

I don't understand why loving Sam and Sam loving me doesn't keep the sun shining for me. I thought when I found my true love, my life would miraculously become perfect. But ever since the earthquake I've had trouble sleeping. I'm awakened by headaches and bad dreams and can't go back to sleep. Here I am so happy with Sam, and yet so fearful.

Last night was the worst yet. I woke up in tears. That's never happened before. I feel so sad and sorry for myself. Poor Molly . . . nine times out of ten, the nightmares include Gotham City-like buildings, crumbling from the top, floor upon floor. What happens before and after changes from dream to dream, but the scenes are violent: Sara buried, Sam sinking in quick sand, me running in place to save them. I awaken at 2:00, 3:00 or 4:00 a.m. out of breath and out of time. In one dream, Sam and I fell and fell, hands held until we lost our grip; we fell apart. I called his name, over and over.

These days I'm walking around my office in a daze. I'm ashamed that I've become so agitated with everyone. I'm afraid my irritability will spill over onto Sam, too.

What's the matter with me? Maybe I need to listen to Kay and talk to a professional. I can't go on this way looking for groundhogs.

Journal
Making of a Love Story

The earthquake had really shaken things up inside me, as well as outside in the physical world. And yet, I fell in love that night. Nothing could stop Sam and me. Not even a killer earthquake. We felt as high as falling in love can take you. Really high. Nine stories high.

Falling wasn't hard. We were protected on all sides, cushioned by passion. It didn't matter if we landed on our feet, our faces, or our asses. We were in love. This was it. *I* was "the One." *He* was "the One." We were both Irish, funny and bright. We were eaters, drinkers and poets. We were dancers and singers. At moments I wondered if we would break under the weight of it.

Even the earth was glad. I could tell because it was unseasonably warm. The moon shone strong, a bold witness to our new young love. The Santa Ana winds, the seductive "Santa Ana's," creating an atmosphere of exotic danger against the backdrop of the landscape.

From our ninth story hotel window, our hearts burst open over the fantastic expanse of Twentieth Century Fox Studios. The sets and stories at the studios could not compare to this love affair we were creating. We were the actors, the directors and producers. We were the writers without any editors. We were making a love story. We were going to live and love forever.

Journal
Phone Conversation after 1st Lunch with Kay

In hopes that Kay could quell my mushrooming fears, I called and admitted, "You know, I'm keeping a pair of running shoes by my bed – ready to run out of the house in the middle of the night. Any shaking still scares me and the four-point aftershocks are enough to remind me of what Sam and I went through on the 9th floor of the Lunamare Hotel."

Kay responded, "Your fear is understandable. I feel lucky that Nick and I chose to live in Pacific Palisades."

"You mean because the Palisades is built on bedrock? Some of our friends just a few miles from here in West L.A had windows blown out, walls and chimneys collapse. Fortunately no one was badly hurt, but when Sam and I walked to my house right after the earthquake, Sara and the neighbors on the street were so relieved to see us.

"You know Kay, Sam was great the night of the quake. I was a wreck. He took over and kept calming me down – reassuring me he would take care of me – telling me we are safe and well. Sam lives not far from the hotel, so he wanted to pass by his house to check on Clancy, his Labrador retriever. When he saw Sam, Clancy was so excited he jumped into Sam's arms and nearly knocked him over. I imagine Clancy thought he would never see Sam again.

Amazingly, there was no damage inside Sam's house. The brick chimney fell, knocking down part of Clancy's back fence. Sam put him on a leash, and we quickly set out for my house. I was hoping I would be lucky, too, and that Sara would be ok, but my anxiety was becoming unbearable.

Once I knew Sara was safe, I broke down and sobbed. I'm not sure Sam understood my fears but he knew I needed him."

Softly Kay said, "Well, Molly love, you sure lived through a nightmare! When I've gone through fearful and dramatic times, I don't think Nick understood my fears. I'm just learning to understand them myself. Now I understand how I created stories of doom and gloom. Since I'm feeling less fearful, Nick thinks I'm much easier to live with."

"How has that happened?" Molly asked.

"Well, Dr. Holman has taught me to look inside myself instead of outside myself. Do you remember how I used to blame Nick and expect him to make me happy?"

Molly answered, "Yes – you are definitely happier. It's interesting, as we talk I can see that even though I'm so in love with Sam, there are times that I do blame him and he sure hates it.

Since we are talking on this level, I have another disturbing problem I'd like to talk about. Since the earthquake, I dread going to sleep. At first I was awakened with just fear symptoms (anxiety, shaking, crying) and now I'm having nightmares – of losing all of the people I love. It's gotten so bad that I try staying awake as long as I can. I feel like a zombie at the office."

"Oh Molly, I see you're suffering. Would you like to see my Dr. Holman? He's an expert on love and fear."

Molly answered, "I know we talked about this before, but I thought I could work it out. If the doctor would see me, perhaps I could get some relief."

Journal
Second Lunch with Kay (About Session 1)

I am a creature of habit. For years Kay and I have met at least once a week for lunch at our same French *café*. As I was waiting for her, I was reminiscing about being there a week earlier with Sam. Since he'd finished a tough script, we were both in high spirits. Our cuddling and cooing caused some to stare disapprovingly but I didn't give a hoot. Molly the teenager was there in full rebellion and Sam adores Molly the teenager. Judgmental glances from other diners only fanned the fire.

I was smiling over my new love when Kay rushed in, bright-eyed and late as usual. We kissed and hugged like long-lost lovers, like the "lovers" we've been since the day we met, some thirty-odd years ago.

It feels great to love someone so thoroughly! I wish I'd had such a relationship with my own mother.

Kay couldn't hold herself back long enough for pleasantries and demanded to know how I thought the session went and how I liked Dr. Holman.

Dr. Holman was nothing like I thought he would be. I saw a six-foot man with a head full of stark white hair and a red face with a sonorous voice. He shook my hand warmly and in a sonorous voice invited me to sit down. I sank into an olive green, down stuffed chair that billowed around me. The late afternoon sun was coming through the brown plantation shutters highlighting miniature orchids.

Dr. Holman sat across from me and to my surprise, took off his shoes, pushed the brown leather ottoman between our chairs, put his feet up and gestured for me to do the same if I wished.

He smiled and said, "Molly? If I may call you Molly?"

"Yes," Molly responded.

"What would you like to get out of our time together?"

"Well... Ummm. I don't know. My best friend Kay encouraged me to come to see you because I'm having nightmares that awaken me in a breathless sweat. Now I'm afraid to go to sleep."

Then I found myself describing the night of the earthquake. It all came out in a flood. I would have expected myself to censor the details, but I just blurted it all out. I told him everything Sam and I did that night, including all of my sexual antics. Since I was less inhibited that night than I've ever been in my life, I was surprised that I could talk to him so easily. There was something about Dr. Holman helped me to feel free. He helped me look at things in a new way. He explained how we all have voices or critics in our heads judging our behavior. In order to feel free and to have a good time, I had been using alcohol to put my "inner critics" to sleep, to free myself from those old critical voices. I couldn't have allowed myself to have that much fun if I hadn't put those critics to sleep. I understand more about how my Catholic upbringing *still* has an effect on me. It's like unveiling a mystery. It's amazing to find out that I'm still in the grip of those black-winged swans."

Kay agreed, telling me that she also believed the nuns had cast a dark spell of prohibition over her sexuality for many years until she got into good therapy like I'm doing now.

Well, the most important part was at the end when I was telling Dr. Holman about the actual earthquake. I began to feel afraid. It was uncanny: my heart started pounding and I could hardly breathe. It was as if it were happening again, then and there.

Dr. Holman believes that when people don't know what to do with their fear or anger, they stuff those feelings into a "reservoir" and shut the lid. The feelings may come out when the time is right. I didn't realize my nightmares were coming out of my experiences in the earthquake. Now it has been long enough afterwards that I am feeling safer, and yet my feelings of terror are starting to come up again in my nightmares. Because I didn't know how to deal with the fear of losing Sara and Sam in the earthquake, he believes that I unconsciously held down the fears. All of this was a big "Aha!" for me.

"There's more," Molly explained to Kay. "Before I left the session he suggested that before I go to sleep I try to turn one of my scary nightmares into a good story. At first it was hard, but when I got into a good fantasy about Sam and me, I amazed myself. I put us on a tropical island, with Sam kissing me all over as the sun set."

Kay and I lifted our glasses together and clinked in laughter and high spirits, saying, "Here's to our sexy fantasies!"

Session #2
Bad Dreams about Sam and Charlie

Dr. Holman opens the waiting room door.

M: (As she enters the office and sits in a chair she is saying…) I couldn't wait to get here. There's still something going on in my dreams. I'm so sad in them. I'm still waking up crying.

H: Would you like to tell me about the dreams?

M: In one dream, I got mad at my brother Charlie, who died in a car accident when I was 17. In the dream, he had fallen in love with a thin, underline "thin," beautiful girl. I was still a round, underline "round," adolescent. I tried to get his attention in the dream, but he kept walking away.

H: How are you feeling as you're remembering the dream?

M: I feel jealous…I feel frustrated that I can't reach him. I feel helpless. I don't know what to do. I also feel scared that someone has come between us. I keep trying to reach him, but I can't. You know, Dr. Holman, I have a lot of dreams about losing people I love. I'm remembering when I was in love with my former husband, Andy, and then the love disappeared. That's happened to me a few times since. Now I'm wondering what will happen with Sam.

H: Do you feel that you're helpless about making things turn out the way you want them to?

M: Absolutely!

H: Do you wonder if there might be something going on inside of you that keeps you from getting what you want?

M: It's hard for me to tell if it's something inside of me that ruins my relationships. It seems as if the trouble starts on the outside.

H: In therapy, we have an opportunity to spend time focusing on what's going on inside of you. I can help you with that. What I'd like to see happen is for you to be at peace inside, within yourself. Then I believe you'll be able to have more of what you want on the outside with the people you love.

M: I'd like that. So how do I get there?

H: Alright! Let's look in a little more detail at the inside.   Let's look at your feelings and beliefs that may influence what happens in your relationship with Sam.

M: Okay.

H: Perhaps a good place to start is with your sad dreams.

M: Alright. Here's one I'd like to look at. I had a dream that Sam left me for Michelle Pfeiffer. I felt such hurt as I watched them walking away from me, holding hands.

H: And it feels very real to you?

M: Yes. Even now the dream is very clear. I can see Sam's face lit by the bright rays from the sun. He was beaming at Michelle as she was looking up, mooning into Sam's handsome face. I felt such a burning jealousy.

H: So that jealousy seems like an old feeling?

M: Oh yes. I know that feeling.

H: Remember last time when we talked about a dream as a   story that you create on the inside, without being aware that you're the creator?

M: Yes, when I realized I was the creator, I changed a bad   dream into a sexy fantasy with Sam.

H: Now that you know you're the dreamer, you know it's possible to re-dream a dream and control what happens. Would like to turn *this* bad dream into a good one?

M: (Laughing) This is going to be fun. Okay,   this   time after Michelle flirts and whispers to him, my Dream-Sam will say, "I'm afraid it's too late, Michelle. I'm already in love with a   beautiful   and fascinating woman."

H: And how do you feel in the new dream-story?

M: (Molly is beaming) I feel euphoric. I feel loved and   loving instead of scared and jealous.

H: Is it clear to you that this change in feelings is due to   changes you made on the inside?

M: Yes. Changing the dream does make it easier for me   to understand that it's not about the Sam on the outside. Now I feel more in charge of myself. I can't believe how my negative feelings in my dream made me feel cool and removed toward my dear, innocent Sam.

H: It was no small thing you did.

Journal After Session #2
Sam Meets Kay and Nick

Tonight, Sam and I went to Kay and Nick's house for dinner. Driving up their driveway, I felt young and free, taking my boyfriend home to meet Mom and Dad. I don't think I've ever felt that way. I don't remember ever taking a boyfriend home to dinner or home for anything. Quite the opposite: I hid them from my parents and my parents from the boys. So when I saw Kay outside, apron over long peasant skirt, cutting roses, waiting for us with her warm welcoming smile, I thought I'd died and gone to heaven. And he was as excited as I was.

Kay is unique – the same age as my mother, but aeons younger, worlds younger; time and space have no measure where Kay is concerned. I love her seventy year old youth and vitality, her ability to be moved, touched, excited – just like me, her little girl. Then Nick came out in the waning winter sun, all scrubbed and smiling. He greeted Sam with a fatherly handshake. I knew I'd struck gold, I'd found my match, my soul mate – and I could see my "parents" approved without hesitation!

My old way was to worry that Kay and Nick wouldn't approve. Dr. Holman has helped me to understand that worry is just a negative story with a bad outcome.

When Sam and Kay started cooking together, my heart was close to bursting. Sam is facile in the kitchen, casual. Kay is careful. She pays attention to detail. The two of them leaned into each other-- allowing, sharing -- Sam cracking jokes, grabbing my ass, giving me random kisses, coddling eggs, tossing Caesar salad, flipping crepes, whipping cream, and intermittently pulling me to him.

It was a mix of many fantasies: mother, lover, food, family, communion, so much love in that warm little kitchen.

Journal Session #3
How Sam and Molly Met

Dear Dr. Holman,

I'm so attracted to Sam. I feel swept away by my love for him. I can't be stopped. No matter what conflicts we get into, they take a backseat to the wonderful loving I experience with Sam.

But I do have a worry. It seems like sex is more important to him than it is to me. When Sam wants to have sex, I feel like only *his* wish counts, even though I want to have sex too. I've had this growing concern for a few months now, since the first night we met, but I'm not sure what to do.

I so love our story, Sam's and mine. I love telling it, hearing him tell it, re-living it each time.

Sam and I met at an exciting Christmas party in Malibu. Our meeting had all the drama of a B movie; high-end party, a few big names, everything Martha-Stewart perfection. Our eyes met momentarily while he chatted with another woman. I looked away, pretending interest in a puffy-faced drunk. He moved around the party like a pro: talking easily, warmly to men and women alike. I watched him. Later, he said that I was never out of his view either; he just couldn't find a worthy approach.

But Fate stepped in, as the three fates always do, tossing out and thus unwinding their ball of yarn, our destinies, just enough for us to grab hold. I had come from the ladies room; he was headed toward the bar; the hall was narrow. The melodramatic music rises to a fever pitch, the young man fumbles, the girl tries to keep composure. The eyes, it was all in the eyes; the immediate attraction, the sweet power of inexplicable desire.

We left the party, a mutual decision, and headed for nearby Moonshadows, drank champagne, ate caviar and talked until they closed.

When we drove up in front of my house, we were high on champagne, life, love, lust and the belief that the "pursuit of happiness" was within reach. We were kissing in the car for who-knows-how-long. When I pulled myself away and explained that my daughter and her babysitter were asleep inside, I felt sure he would understand why I wasn't inviting him in. I gave him a kiss full of promise before I got out of the car, leaning in to whisper, "Goodnight."

Sam didn't get it. He jumped out of the car, and all the way to my front door, he pressured me to let him inside, literally and figuratively. He wanted what we both wanted, but I wasn't going to risk getting caught. While I told him I had to think of my daughter, he was reaching underneath my sweater, not listening to a word. Although I could feel him pressing against my thigh, I was resolute. If Sara awakened in the night, it would be very upsetting for all of us. None of my arguments worked. Ultimately, he left feeling hurt or rejected or both. I didn't think I'd ever see him again.

The next evening when he called, I felt relieved to hear his voice and I felt guilty for pushing him away. But I was right, wasn't I? Wouldn't any mother want to protect her child from such a shocking scene?

As we talked, he revealed that he *did* have second thoughts about calling me back. *That* got my attention! He said, "It wasn't only that I didn't get what I wanted, but your righteousness really turned me off." He alluded to previous experiences, "and if I hadn't remembered how great I felt with you, I probably wouldn't have called."

My heart hit the floor when I heard him say he almost didn't call me. I was taken aback! I didn't know what to say. I felt so certain about my point of view as a parent that I didn't see it as a rigid stance.

Dr. Holman, is there any substance to Sam's comments? Do I come across as self-righteous in other parts of my life – with Sara, my mother, at work?

Well, who is *he*, after all? He doesn't even have any children. *I'm* her parent. *I* know what's right for Sara!

Don't you agree with me, Dr. Holman?

Molly

Session #3
Holly Reads Journal to Dr. Holman – The Critics

(After Molly reads her journal to Dr. Holman.)

M: So what do you think of all that? Do you think I was right?

H: Actually, I don't believe in right and wrong. I think the "Right Wrong Game" is used by people who are critical or judgmental to get you over to their side. Most of us aren't aware of the fall-out. But let's look at that night from the inside out. If you set yourself up as right, what do you think Sam feels?

M: Let me think a minute... Well, it's possible Sam could feel that I was pushing him away, when actually *I* didn't want him to leave either.

H: What I sense going on in you that night was a lot of sexual excitement and pleasure. I'm wondering what went into making the decision to stop.

M: I had a twelve-year old pre-adolescent daughter in the house. Are you suggesting that I go into my house and make love at midnight with a man neither Sara nor I know, and take the risk that Sara could awaken and burst in on us? Who knows what that could do to her...

H: I understand your wish to protect Sara from possible harm if she should discover you having sex. That point of view is certainly widely held. There are also a few dissenting opinions. However, what's important is *your* opinion.

I'm curious about how you arrived at your position? It must have been very hard for you, having finally found your dream man, to send him away at the height of your passion and on the verge of fulfillment. The strength that you needed in order to stop was considerable.

M: I never imagined that anyone could behave otherwise.

H: Suppose people are not born with the belief that sex or viewing sex can be harmful?

M: I never thought of it that way. Where did I get such a strong belief? I guess it was my parents or the nuns that taught me, and I never doubted it. I like your idea that it's my opinions that are important.

H: Do you want to follow that idea back into the car with Sam, where you voted to stop your sexy feelings?

M: Okay...first I feel the thrill of that night, until he started pushing me to let him in my house! He was insistent about finishing what we had started. It felt like he was being selfish. All he thought about was himself... and sex.

H: Is that the way your parents or the nuns would look at it?

M: Yes.

H: So it's understandable that they would vote for you to stop, and you voted with them.

M: I did? I guess I did!

H: There seem to be more than two people in Sam's car.

M: (Molly laughs) My parents and the nuns?

H: Those people in your bed are what I call "the critics." Critics are the important people in your life who tell you what you should or shouldn't do. They told you their ideas about sexuality, and you agreed so thoroughly that you weren't aware those were *their* ideas. Your own ideas never had a chance to form. I have another word I like to use: "the teller." The nuns and your parents *told* you what was right and wrong. In addition, their attitudes were often critical and threatening. If you didn't agree with them, maybe bad things would happen to you. I call them "critics" or "tellers" because they state that there's something wrong or bad about *you.*

M: I know those voices. I heard them in the confessional, on the playground, at the dinner table, everywhere. I still hear them. So, are you saying that night when I gave up having sex with Sam, because I was afraid of what they, "the critics" would say?

Molly pauses.

M: So, is it possible Sara could be one of my critics? In fact, she's one of my *worst* critics.

H: I'm confused about Sara being one of your critics. What is your history with Sara?

M: Since Andy and I divorced, my relationship with Sara has changed. She blames me for the divorce, and I defend myself, and then she gets so mad it's scary. So you can see why I wouldn't want to risk taking a strange man into my home and into my bed and risk Sara seeing me in a compromised position. I'm realizing how afraid I am of Sara judging me.

H: So your anger at Sam is really a cover story for your fear of Sara's judgment and anger.

M: Hmmmmmm . . .

H: Next time you come in, if it's okay with you, I'd like to talk about my thoughts on anger. Anger is not bad or good. I see anger as a signal. It signals, for instance, that you gave up your pleasure with Sam in order to be in good standing with your daughter.

Journal #1 After
Session #3

After my session, I decided to talk to Sam. I recognized what a pill I had been that night in the car. I was self-righteous, knowing I was doing the right thing for Sara, not seeing my own inner conflict about sex, not recognizing that I was pushing Sam away.

I asked Sam if he remembered that night we first met, sitting together in the car in front of my house? *I* was struggling to be a good single mother. I wanted to compensate for my mom's lack of concern, for how she allowed me to raise myself. And there *he* was, an attractive stranger attempting to seduce me. I was not going to let him influence me away from my beliefs, making me feel like a bad mother. I admitted it, I was stuck on being right.

I then explained to Sam that since seeing Dr. Holman, I've discovered that I'm afraid of Sara's anger. That was the problem the other night also.

Sam said he was confused. Here he finds this sexy woman who's been all over him and when he gets to her house, she stops him cold. He told me how frustrated he was by the time he left, something I already knew and didn't care about at the time.

Sam said, "Boy, you are one complicated woman. But I must admit, I'm intrigued."

When I leaned over and kissed his soft, warm lips, I knew I would have felt like a fool if I'd lost him.

Journal #2 After Session #3
What Do I Want?

Dr. Holman and I had an intimate talk about my sexual attitudes. It was obvious that I have been severely influenced by the big authorities, the head honchos of the church. Mom and Dad made it very clear how they wanted their precious daughter to follow both the nuns' and the school's explicit attitudes about "our girls" and sex.

Of course Mom and Dad kept their hawk eyes on me from age thirteen. So why *wouldn't* I have these strict inner rules about sex? When Holman told me the important thing was what *I* wanted, then I boldly said, "Good, let's find out."

Now I'm wondering, "What *do* I want? How do I find out what I want?"

Session #4
Invisible Judges/Sun Bathing

M: Let me tell you about something that happened this weekend that got me thinking about your "critics." As you know, it was unseasonably beautiful on Saturday. As I was sunbathing I was aware of how good I felt, inside and out. The sun felt so nourishing on my body. No one was in the yard; no one could see me. I was in complete privacy. But after a while, I began to feel uncomfortable. I began to cover up. I pulled my towel over my legs. A few minutes later, I put the towel over my stomach, then I realized what I was doing. Who was I hiding from? I was hiding from me! From myself, Dr. Holman. It was scary. I didn't like what I saw.

That's when I remembered our talking about critics. I wondered if I'd encountered one while I was sitting in the sun. Then I remembered thinking that Sam might drop by. I realized that remote possibility motivated my covering up.

H: It seems like a good example of what I call an "invisible judge". At first the idea of anyone seeing you naked was beneath the level of your consciousness. The judges did their work, as if Sam were there in person.

M: I get it. It wasn't even the real Sam. It was *my* image of him. And I even put my judges' eyes in his head and their words in his mouth: "She's ugly and fat and I don't want a woman like that."

H: Sounds like you're making your automatic thoughts and actions conscious.

M: I did do that, didn't I? (pause) But what do I do with the information?

H: Since you see that you created this image of Sam, you might like to try creating another image. Close your eyes for a moment. Let's try Take Two. Create an image of Sam who is not only approving but also desirous of you as you are.

M: Okay, I'm working on it . . .

(They are silent for awhile.)

H: Sam's standing before you, he pulls you up, wrapping you in his arms. What would you like him to say? Isn't it surprising? Nothing has changed in the Outer World. But you have deliberately changed your unconscious belief about the invisible judge and now you   feel unashamed.

M: I see! If I could create the negative story that he would see me and think me unacceptable, then I could just as easily create an accepting Sam, a Sam that loves me as I am – and wants me as I am.

But I'm so used to thinking the first way, the old way. It's familiar. But that wasn't so hard. But I'm afraid it would take years to acquire the ability to do it this way – the positive way.

H: Regarding the consensual belief that fat is ugly and thin is beautiful, you know, of course, the famous painter of nude women, Renoir, loved fleshiness. It was the style at the time. There is no absolute measure of physical beauty, just consensus of society.

M: That's a hard one. I'm caught up in our current view of thinness and beauty.

H: Soon you may want to experiment with the idea that you do not give permission or support to anyone who judges you. Of course, people in the Outer World may judge you, but knowing what you know now, you don't have to endorse either their right to judge you or the judgment itself. Negative judgments by others are not about you; they're expressions of hidden anger directed at you. These judgments come from inside of *them*. You can say "Thanks, but no thanks. I am no longer willing to be the target of your judgment."

M: I can I do that, I think.

H: Beliefs are stories you tell yourself. As you just found out, you can change your beliefs by changing your stories.

Look what happened to Cinderella. Her sisters and stepmother believed she was "less-than" worthy to go to the Prince's ball. However, if Cinderella did not have a Fairy Godmother, she would never have gone to the Ball and met the Prince. She would have indeed felt unworthy. That means she unconsciously agreed that those people like her sisters and stepmother, who directed anger toward her by putting her down, were right. They were the "critics committee." The only one who did not agree that Cinderella deserved to be the target of their subtle anger or judgments was the Fairy Godmother. When she presented Cinderella with her view that she was worthy, Cinderella changed her vote in agreement. And you know the rest of the story . . . they lived happily ever after.

M: Well, that's what I'm after – living happily ever after. Sounds like Fairy Godmothers are good people to have around. Are you my Fairy Godmother?

H: (Bursts out laughing.) Well, okay, perhaps for a while, until you learn how to be your own Fairy Godmother and to create your own coach and horses.

M: Wow, that sounds like magic! I can't wait!

H: The magic lies in reclaiming your own power to create positive images and outcomes.

Session #5
Stallion Dream – Passion and Punishment

M: I had a powerful dream. I even wrote it down in the middle of the night. May I read it to you?

H: Please.

M: I'm riding a wild stallion up the side of a mountain. I'm on my way to meet my lover. I feel exhilarated. Suddenly, a black cloud rushed toward me. I'm afraid the horse might be startled from the thunder and lightening. I'm afraid that I'll be thrown from the horse and killed.

The trail is unfamiliar. Up ahead, on the mountainside, I see a dead tree, branches stretching over the trail, the kind of tree that vultures usually wait in often. The wind picks up and blows the raindrops diagonally, stinging my face.

I feel such dread. I fear something terrible is about to happen. The horse is relentless, moving toward the dead tree. I try to rein him in, screaming inaudibly. He keeps going! I'm terrified of reaching that tree, all black, looking as if it were burnt by lightning in years past. The branches are arms, reaching out with bony fingers, impatient for me to come close. And the stallion, moving inexorably toward that tree, totally against my will, ignores my tight pull on the reins.

As I yell, "Help! Help!" suddenly I think I hear a voice whispering in my ear.

(Molly looks up from reading.) Maybe it was your voice.

(He smiles and she continues reading.)

I can't remember the words, but the message is clear: "Use your power. Change the story."

In a split second, I determine to overcome my fear. I flatten my body against the stallion and dig my heels into his sweaty flanks. As his legs extend, we surge forward as one, passing right by the tree. I start to cry with gratitude and relief as I put my arms around his powerful neck, nuzzling my face into the damp heat of his mane. We made it! We made it!

I wake up with my heart pounding, my hair and nightgown drenched from exertion and fear and excitement. I feel like I've surrendered my body to the most powerful sexual feelings I've ever experienced.

H: What a dream! It sounds like you made a breakthrough. By overcoming your fear of losing control, by opening up to the sexual power . . .

M: I think so too. I had an epiphany! Such pleasure broke through all my repressed sexuality. Like a flood bursting through a dam!

H: Yes, the good feelings came *bursting* through! (They laugh together.) I notice you don't reach your lover in the dream. You're almost there. Would you like to finish the dream?

M: Sure.

H: Close your eyes. (Silence. A few minutes go by. When she opens her eyes, she has the biggest smile on her face.)

M: I'm so grateful to you, Dr. Holman, even in my dream you were there to help me. I never expected to feel so wonderful from a dream. It's been with me all day.

H: I've found that the feelings we experience in a dream, good or bad, can certainly affect how we feel the next day.

M: In my dream, I worked so hard to get to the good feelings, I'd like to *stay* with the pleasure.

H: (Smiles and nods.) It feels so good to feel good, I've often wondered why we don't do it *all* the time?

Journal After Session #5
Mexican Dinner

Tonight, after my session with Holman, I felt like I had just climbed a mountain and reached the peak. I felt exhilarated, breathing the cool, thin, mountain air. I wanted to share my magnificent dream with Sam, but I was not sure he shared my feelings that dreams and therapy are important. After all, I'm just realizing myself that therapy is a lifelong process of learning how to make changes so we can be happy and fulfilled.

Sam and I are committed to each other, and yet these childlike, unsafe feelings seem to interfere with my self-confidence and the love I feel for and from him.

Maybe I should never have had that margarita with our Mexican dinner because it loosened my tongue. I revealed the excited feeling I had in my dream riding the black stallion up the mountain.

Sam came back with, "I wish you shared that sexual excitement with *me*." Of all my concerns about sharing, I had never considered this one. I felt my temper flare, but remembered Dr. Holman's hot potato theory just in time. I took Sam's hand in mine and said, "Behind your complaint is your wish." Looking at him coyly, I asked, "How can you facilitate your wish?"

Sam's eyes brightened. "I have a few ideas, but we can't do any of them here in the restaurant." Without a word, we both slid out of the booth.

Session #6
Critics and Pleasure

At 5:00 in the evening, I walked into Dr. Holman's office and told him I had experienced the most perfect morning of my life. Then I blushed a deep red and covered my face with my hands.

M: One part of me wants to tell you about my erotic morning. Another part is afraid of what you may think of me.

H: Molly, did you notice what just happened? As you say, at one moment you were remembering a pleasurable experience. Then, in a flash, you were feeling afraid and embarrassed. What do you think was going on inside?

M: You're right. My feelings did change suddenly from excitement to embarrassment. I was reacting as if you would judge me. The way I would feel with my parents. I consider them prudes--, I wouldn't feel comfortable sitting here telling my father, for instance. But I realize you're not my daddy, so here goes, I'll tell you.

Sam slept over. Sara, Sam, and I had a delicious breakfast, thanks to Sam. He made Sara's favorite, blueberry pancakes.

As soon as Sara left for school, Sam started to take off my robe. He began kissing me from my shoulders down. I started giggling--I loved his playfulness. Then he pulled me toward the bedroom and started making love to me slowly and gently.

I realized from my lack of sensation that I wasn't into it. I was feeling anxious. When I told Sam how I was feeling, he ran a hot bubble bath for me, lathering each part of my body with the big bath sponge. I was starting to feel very turned on when the clock struck eight. I should have been walking out the front door.

Sam quickly dried and powdered my body, tickling me with a maribou duster. We felt gleeful, like truant school children. Then my anxiety surfaced again, and I dressed in five minutes flat.

Before I ran out of the house, I pushed Sam against the front door, covering his face with kisses. I told him how much I loved him.

I put the top down on my convertible and sang with the radio all the way to work.

Now, here's the thing. I wonder why I didn't feel free enough to stay there and fully enjoy the pleasure. I could have called work to say I was coming in late. After all, I am the senior editor. I could be late once in a while.

H: Was there anyone else in the room with you and Sam?

M: Heavens no! Why do you ask?

H: Was your daddy watching you this morning with Sam?

M: Oh! No wonder I couldn't get aroused! (They both laugh.) I'm beginning to see how those nosey critics spoil my pleasure. In my family, sex was *never* discussed. I know both my parents agreed with the Catholic Church: Sex outside of marriage is a mortal sin, you know. It must have been very important for me to be Daddy's good little girl since I wore pigtails and kept my baby fat through high school. It wasn't until I left home for college that I lost my virginity. I never realized how much power I gave my father to keep me from having pleasure. And all this time, I thought I was so *free* sexually!

Journal 1 After Session #6
Sexual Fears

Talking about sexuality with Dr. Holman today was great, even though I had a hard time getting started. My excitement doesn't come from titillation but from the feeling that I think we, I, made some progress.

For now, progress means understanding myself more clearly. Today I had glimpses into the relationship between my developing self and my developing sexuality.

I'm sitting here with questions emerging from our conversation today. What happens to all the memories of the past forty-something years? Must I carry my mother and father and brother and old lovers into my bed every night? Is there a way for them not to be watching and judging me when I'm having sex? Or are they a necessary part of it? Is sex really a group affair? How do I transform this family of critics into allies? Can I study sex, Dr. Holman, so I'll get better at it?

Before Sam, I was an actress. I performed but no one knew it. It worked well enough for my partners. But for me, the real story leaked out in spurts of withdrawal, tiredness and the proverbial headache. Was I unconsciously creating situations that precluded sex? Before any sexual interlude, I'd suddenly be starving, craving Rice Krispies with milk and brown sugar. Or I'd say, "I'll be right back," and rush to the bathroom, compelled by a need to be cleaner, more sweet-smelling for my lover. Other times, I'd feel I just had to have a shot of vodka first. Or watch the eleven o'clock news.

Here I was, trying to be this sex goddess, an earthly Aphrodite who was supposed to love sex. Who had, after all, fallen in love finally and who seemed to know what she was doing. Really, I just wanted to take my football and go home. Put on my flannel pajamas and read a book. But wasn't I in love? Isn't love sacrifice? Isn't true love shown by pleasing your man?

Why didn't I question the fact that I wasn't having such a good time? What was I afraid of? While sitting with Dr. Holman, I had the courage to ask myself questions. Where did these fears come from? Fear of showing my body, of being criticized, of not pleasing him and him and him. Fear of my own pleasure. Fear of not being loved. What if I had understood years ago that I created the fear stories and then believed them? Or that I was trying to remain in good standing with my critics-- my parents, the nuns, the society at large.

Instead, what if the critics had tried to please *me*? That thought brings a smile to my face, opens a door to pleasure. Imagine the difference if I had spoken truthfully to a lover, if I had asked him for what I wanted. (And what he wanted.)

That's the way I want to be with Sam.

Journal 2 After Session #6
Mammoth Mountain

If there is a God, She is with me now! The weekend with Sam turned out beautifully. All I had to do was show up with my cute winter togs and my willingness to enjoy! Another dream come true – a man who can take charge of romance, who can initiate, and then follow through. Although we had a fight on the way up, the resolution and lovemaking later made it all worthwhile. I'm blown away by this man.

On the way up to Mammoth, his driving scared me. It was bad enough on the freeway, but when we started wending our way up the snowy, snaky road, I began to panic. My head filled with nightmares that the reason we were going to Mammoth was that we were going to die. "The earthquake didn't get us, so this is how we'll die," I thought. My mind went crazy and I was petrified. I asked him to slow down. When he didn't, I pleaded louder. He got mad, I got mad. He pointed that damned finger and said, "There you go again with that righteous tone of voice." I got quiet, wondering if he were right, but with the rapidly passing twists and turns, fear mounted to the point I thought I might cry. I didn't want to ruin everything and I know how sensitive he is to my telling him what to do, but my racing mind had me convinced that we would slide off the edge into the abyss below, hundreds of feet of snow and sure death. When I spoke again, my voice was angrier. "Why are you so stubborn? Can't you hear that I'm afraid? Fear isn't negotiable. Stop driving like a maniac!"

He reacted to my anger by pulling over and telling me to drive. I begged off, refusing to move out of the passenger's seat. Then he got really mad, yelling about my being bossy and controlling. I turned into stone. We sat there at an impasse as big as the mountain. Fortunately, it got so cold that it melted his stubbornness. He started the car and drove in silence all the way to the cabin.

I tried to make nice-nice as we unpacked, but he would have none of it. Spreading a quilt in front of the fire, I set up the incredible picnic *he* had packed: Whole Foods' rotisserie chicken and honey-mustard ribs, garlic-roasted potatoes in sea salt, asparagus marinated in balsamic vinegar and olive oil, ciabatta, grilled and buttered, and an incredible chilled Viognier; it was a lovers' feast. Even down to the cloth napkins, the wine goblets and the votive candles. But he still would have none of it, and none of me. We ate in silence.

I got fed up and went for a walk toward Mollie's, a little bar in town. He was behind me, but I didn't know it. I walked into the lounge and sat down at the bar. After a while when he came up from behind and asked me to dance, I melted into his strong arms, tired and needing to collapse. We said nothing, just held each other, listened to the other's breathing. I realized how precious life is, how precious *he* is – a man with a heart, a man who feels things, a body and mind that responds. "We are alive," I rejoiced. "Don't waste these moments."

I'm learning from Dr. Holman that if I have the imagination to make it up, I have the imagination to unmake it. It was as though Sam and I were each oppressed by our own stories, coming out in anger toward each other. Thank heaven I had the power to change mine.

I decided to talk to Sam on our walk home. I gathered my courage, leading him from the dance floor. I was a bit nervous to articulate something I'd really just learned myself.

Holding Sam by the hand, I looked back to see if his eyes were saying yes or no. I think he thought I was taking him back to the cabin to seduce him. His eyes said yes. When we got out into the freezing night air, our breath steaming like trains, I said that I thought our argument could have been precluded if – he cut me off. "Do we have to discuss *everything*? I'm tired of analyzing. Let's just drop it."

"Wait, please, Sam, just one minute . . . when I was scared today, driving up here, I made up a story that we would slide in the ice and go careening off the steep cliff. My fear carried me away. Maybe it's a hangover from the earthquake, I don't know. Anyway, I made you the culprit, saying you were driving crazy and too fast, and I'm really sorry. Sam, my sweet Sam, I see that I put you in a box canyon with all that fear and blame. Can you forgive me?"

Sam couldn't believe his ears. If the look on his face was any indication, I had not only said it clearly, but he'd understood what I'm just beginning to get. I felt so good at that moment, so strong, so smart, so sexy. I threw my arms around him, thanking him for being who he is. Then I dragged him back into the cabin.

True communication like that is, for me, a turn-on. When there's so much honesty and insight and love attached to the words, and so much effort to speak and hear and understand, I feel it physically, in my belly, and below.

I ripped off his six layers of clothes in a nanosecond and then danced around the cabin, slowly taking mine off, driving him crazy. We were so cold and so hot at the same time, cheeks burning, hands and feet freezing, our excitement in each other beyond what it had ever been. It must be illegal to feel that good. The wine from dinner had probably worn off and I found myself amazed; we were sober and I wasn't hiding. Our lovemaking was just that, lovemaking. I can't remember feeling so close to another human being.

I'm glad that the door to the truth is so wide and that I have the guide of a lifetime – my wizard, Dr. Holman!

Session #7
1ˢᵗ PAR with Sam: Co-fusion of Love/Anger

M: I feel confused today. After our incredible weekend in Mammoth, I don't like feeling this way. I pushed Sam away, yet I wanted him to be close. Let me tell you what happened last night.

H: Let's hear.

M: Well, last night Sara was spending the night at a friend's. Sam and I had big plans. I was looking forward to a sexy evening with a sexy man. We had a lot of fun fooling around in the kitchen while we were cooking. I was imagining the martinis and dinner would be a prelude to the music we would make later.

After dinner, I told Sam I'd meet him in the living room with coffee. And what did I find? Sam had fallen asleep on the couch! I quietly turned back to the kitchen and started the dishes. I kept glancing at him, expecting him to wake up. The longer he slept, the angrier I felt. Then I finally decided to go to bed.

H: And?

M: It was barely light when Sam came and kissed me awake. I didn't feel like kissing him back. He noticed, and asked me what was wrong. I said, "Nothing's wrong." He insisted on knowing, but I kept my cool. In my family it was very important to stay cool. My   mother held her head high and never let on when she was angry. She would never let my father know if he hurt her feelings.

H: So with Sam, when you felt angry and hurt, it made sense to you to hold your feelings in, to "keep your cool."

M: Yes, that's right! I was determined not to let Sam see how irritated I was. He kept insisting that I tell him what was wrong. I just ignored him and started getting dressed. He finally blew up. I guess my attitude pushed one of his hot buttons.

Sam has told me that he hates it when his family has loud, angry fights, which usually happen when his father drinks. But at least they get everything out in the open. So Sam hates the way I "clam up," as he calls it.

I left home this morning maintaining my cool, but now I'm feeling upset.

H: I understand. Could we go back for a second to the part   when Sam was kissing you? Did you want to kiss him back?

M: Yes, but I couldn't.

H: What was stopping you?

M: Well I was angry with him.

H: So you wanted to "keep your cool," like your mother?

M: Yes, that's right.

H: How did that approach work out for your mother?

M: Pretty well, I guess. I never saw her give in, no matter   what my father said or did.

H: What kinds of things did he do?

M: He tried humor, affection, teasing,   clowning. But nothing worked with her. She seemed strong to me, the way she   held   her ground. It felt like she won.

H: So you thought this was a good way to go?

M: Yes. Not only did she win, but she prevented arguments and fights from ever taking place in our family.

H: And how does her approach work for *you*?

M: It's okay, as long as I hold in my anger. As a child, when I wasn't able to hold it in and had a tantrum, my mother called me a two year old, and my father sent me to my room to "get control" of myself.

H: So it worked better for you to hold in your anger?

M: Yes, at home, anyway.

H: And how does this approach work with Sam?

M: Obviously, not very well. He got mad at me this morning.

H: You're saying the old, cool method worked as a child, but   as an adult with Sam, it's not working?

M: I guess you could say that.

H: So you're still left holding in your anger?

M: That's true.

H: Have you considered telling Sam why you're angry?

M: Yes, but so far I've decided not to.

H: What led you to that decision?

M: I'm afraid he'll get mad, I suppose.

H: So, when Sam invites you to tell him what's going on, you feel it isn't safe.

M: That's it exactly! I'm stuck, Dr. Holman! If I'm angry and keep my cool, Sam gets mad at me. But if I do talk about my anger, I'm still afraid he'll get mad at me.

H: I understand your conflict, Molly. What if we had a *safe* way for you to express your anger?

M: Safely express anger? Sounds like a paradox. Is that possible?

H: You know, Molly, this predicament you describe – I've encountered it in so many of my clients. Early on, I began experimenting with methods to resolve the anger. Finally, I designed an exercise that seems to work fairly well. I call it "Pretend Anger Release" or "PAR." It allows you to get your anger out safely, and the beauty of it is, with harm to no one.

M: Really? I'd like to learn how to do that.

H: Good. I've found there's an added bonus. Once you allow yourself to vent anger safely, you are then free to find out what your original good feelings were, the ones that were blocked and gave rise to your anger in the first place.

M: Okay, so how do I do this exercise, this "Pretend Anger Release"?

H: First, you go into your inner world of imagination. Here you create what I call a "Safety Dome" with thick walls through which no one can see or hear. These walls will keep anyone on the outside from hearing or knowing what takes place on the inside. It will be safe for you to say or do anything you want without fear of judgment by anyone outside the walls. How does that sound to you?

M: You mean I can say and do *anything* to Sam?

H: Yes, the purpose of the dome is to physically and verbally release as much anger as you can. It won't hurt you or Sam.

Alright, let's start. I find it helpful to make this statement first. Will you repeat after me?

M: Okay, here I go. (Molly nods and repeats after Holman)

         "I am creating this dome in my inner world of imagination. Inside my dome, nothing I say or do can get through the walls, so that no one on the outside can be harmed or affected in any way. That means that inside my dome I can do or say anything and no one can judge me. Inside the dome, I acknowledge that I am dealing with my own *images* of people, not the people themselves. I am the director of this drama. Everything goes according to my wishes. If I don't like what's happening, I can change it. The purpose of this exercise is first to get my anger out safely, then to go find my hidden treasures."

H: It's important that you say this each time at the beginning of the "PAR."

M: Okay, I understand.

H: As you begin to work with it, each time you make your statement with focused attention, you will get more understanding of the meaning. Now are you ready for the next step?

M: Yes, go ahead.

H: Pretend that you take Sam by the hand. Open the door and lead him inside your Safety Dome. Close the door behind you.

M: Should I shut my eyes?

H: If you like. Now that you're inside, place Sam where you would like him to be. Place yourself. Tune in on your anger feelings toward him. Let yourself *feel* your anger in your body.

M: I'm not feeling as angry as I was. I'll just tell him I'm disappointed about the other night.

H: Can you tell him what you're disappointed about?

M: I'm embarrassed to say it out loud. I'm afraid you'll think I'm terrible if I really get mad at him or say mean things.

H: And I won't like you?

M: Yes. (she smiles.)

H: I understand your concern, Molly, but I'm not here to judge you. And in the dome, no one else can judge you either.

M: Really? Whew! That's a relief.

H: Would you allow yourself to be in the dome now with Sam? Focus on your thoughts, feelings and sensations. What do you sense in your body?

M: My whole chest feels heavy. I feel pulled down by it.

H: Can you go into that place in your chest? Can you sense any emotional feelings there? (He waits.)

M: It feels like . . . hurt.

H: Okay, is there anything else you feel in your body?

M: I feel pressure in my head, a tension in my jaw, like I'm holding something back.

H: Are there any words or images that come to mind?

M: I see myself yelling. Yelling at Sam.

H: In the safety provided by your safety dome, as you're tuning into your feelings, images and body sensations, what would you like to express to Sam? Signal to me when you're finished.

M: (Inhales sharply.) Sam! You stooo-pid idiot! (She grabs him by the shoulders like a rag doll.) You ruined everything! Your naps are so fucking important you don't know what you missed out on. You're a fool. I had planned secret, sexy stuff to lay on you and you had the gall to fall asleep. Two martinis, you're out. You wimp!!! And then you pretend not to know why I'm mad. You really are clueless, you stupid idiot!

(Molly opens her eyes) I think that's it.

H: Do you feel you've gotten all your anger out?

M: Pretty much.

H: And did you feel safe?

M: Safe enough.

H: How are you feeling now?

M: I feel much lighter. I didn't realize how much anger I had stored up in here (Putting her hand over her chest). It feels like I literally got something off my chest. I can finally take a deep breath. (Molly breathes deeply.)

H: Good! Now we are ready for the third step.

M: What's that?

H: Think of the way you'd like Sam to react to what you said and did to him.

M: I'd like him to respond like this: "You're right, Molly. You're absolutely right to say what you said to me and do what you did. I'm so glad you told me your true feelings.

H: How is it when Sam says that to you?

M: (starting to cry) It feels so good for him to accept my feelings . . . to really understand that I have good reason to be mad at him.

H: Would you like for Sam to say how sorry he feels for treating you with such insensitivity?

M: Yes, I would like that: "Molly, I feel so sorry that I spoiled your evening. I deeply regret that I fell asleep. I wish I had stayed awake to give you what you wanted. I'm sorry I caused you so much grief and anger. I wish I could make it up to you."

H: Molly, what do you think? Would you be willing to let Sam make it up to you?

M: (pauses and thinks about it) Yes, I'm willing. Okay, Sam I'm willing!

H: The next step is for Sam to ask you *how* you would like him to make it up to you.

M: Oh, he knows how. I don't have to tell him.

H: Please tell him anyway.

M: Sam, I'd like for you to say, "I'll take a five minute nap and wake up refreshed." Then I want you to jump up from the couch, come over to where I'm washing the dishes, put your arms around me and hold me tight. Nuzzle and kiss me all over the back of my neck.

H: What would you like to happen next?

M: Well, now we'll go ahead with the very intimate evening I was planning.

H: Do you feel Sam has made it up to you now?

M: Yes, indeed! I do! (Big smile, face glowing.)

H: Feeling that way, Molly, look at him. See if you want to forgive him.

M: Yes, I do.

H: Would you like to hug him?

M: Yes, I'd like that. (She closes her eyes and sits silently for a moment.)

        Okay, I truly forgive you.

H: Now, allow yourself to luxuriate in your feelings. Take your time.

M: This feels wonderful, wonderful.

H: Can we say you've found the treasure behind your anger?

M: Oh! I just remembered something important from last night. I had forgotten my fantasy about how I wanted the evening to go.

H: It sounds like having let your anger out has safely cleared the way for more treasure to come out. What was the fantasy?

M: Actually, I had rented the video, *Tango Lesson* and watched it by myself, feeling very excited and turned on. I always wanted to learn to do the tango. It's such a provocative, sexy dance, and Sam is such a good dancer. When I first met Sam, we danced the tango. I melted into the strength of his body. We danced as if we were one. Anyway, after the movie, I rummaged through my grandmother's trunk, looking for something unusual to wear for my dinner with Sam.

        At last I found her black lace gown with a deep V-shaped décolletage. It was a little snug, but I held my breath and zipped it. Her black satin dance slippers fit me perfectly, and the four-inch heels gave me such a svelte look. I could just picture the grin on Sam's face.

        So here's the fantasy. After our special dinner, I'd excuse myself for a few minutes and return as a vision from my grandmother's day. Black lace, Carmen red lips and a scarlet rose freshly picked from my garden, clenched between my teeth. I could hardly wait to play the part. At the end of our dance, we would bow and curtsy to one another, Sam would lift me into the air and light as a feather, roll me onto the bed!

H: That sounds like a very exciting wish. As you're telling it, how do you feel?

M: On cloud nine! It's a delicious, floating feeling. I know I could finish the story now, with my inner world image of Sam, but I'd rather go find my outer world Sam and finish it together.

H: Congratulations, Molly. You started out angry with Sam in a no-win situation. Then you felt as if you were between a rock and a hard place. You turned it into a win-win. All you had to do was find a way to get your anger out safely, without hurting anyone in your outer world.

M: That's what happened, isn't it? It felt so good, releasing my anger in the dome. Then step-by-step, you helped me find my treasure. And now look! I'm back to my loving feelings for Sam. You showed me something new, that there is a way to express anger safely.

Journal #1 After Session #7

Sam's changes are surprising me. After my session with Dr. Holman, I met Sam. He was interested to hear how I changed my "cool anger" to loving feelings and a passionate fantasy. I was relieved that Sam was also curious about the process of my therapy. And he didn't take anything personally. What a change tonight. He told me that he was feeling more in love with me! He believes it's because I'm sharing my feelings and not "blaming him." This new way of talking about ourselves with each other is blowing him away. He told me that he didn't know a love affair could feel this good. I'm so grateful to Dr. Holman. For the first time I have real hope of a lasting relationship.

Journal #2 After Session #7
Dinner for Eight – Inner/Outer World

The next evening, Sam and I were sitting on my porch in bliss having a beer together, giggling and talking.

The phone interrupted us. It was Kay. She and Nick were in the neighborhood and wanted to come by. I told her it was great timing because Sam was here.

Sam rushed to the kitchen and set four glasses in the freezer for beer. He whipped up a spinach dip and shrimp cocktail with crackers and brought them out to the porch. I pushed him into a chair, jumped on his lap and hurried to reward him before they got here.

Ten minutes later we were all laughing and enjoying each other. Sam kissed me, looked at Kay and said with great conviction, " I love her so much, I can't wait to marry her." I was stunned by this public admission.

I moved closer to Sam. I told him that I love his Inner World fantasy, but I've learned from Dr. Holman that there's an Inner World Molly that he creates, and an Outer World Molly that he interacts with. I asked which one he wanted to marry.

Sam made us all laugh when he said, "Schminner World, Schmouter World!" Sam turned and put his arms around me saying, "This is the only Molly I care about."

I picked up my beer glass and toasted him. "Sam, I hope that when you get to know the real me, you'll like me as much as you like your fantasy Molly."

Holding my face in his hands, he asked, "So Molly, are we getting married or not?"

What could I say in front of Kay and Nick? I had to say, "Of course." In fact, I'll invite my mother to have lunch and give her the news.

I love Nick for breaking in just then. He said that speaking of lunch, he was really hungry. Sam offered to whip something up for us to eat on the patio. He poked his head through the kitchen door. "Set the table for eight," he yelled.

"Eight?" I repeated.

He answered smiling, "I'm making enough food for our Inner Selves and our Outer Selves!"

Session #8
Dome with Charlie

M: You know, Dr. Holman, Sam waited until last night to tell me he was leaving tomorrow for a week on location. He's been working on a script the last few months, and now the company wants him there for the filming. Since it's such a remote location, and there's no airport, and it's so hot right now, he's planning to drive all night through the desert and the Sierra Mountains.

As he was telling me his plans, an ice-cold feeling went through me. Things went dark in front of my eyes and for a few moments I lost my equilibrium. I didn't know what was happening.

Flashing through my mind came an awareness of a dark premonition. I was too scared to tell Sam what I was thinking and experiencing for fear of creating a self-fulfilling prophecy. Instead, I acted like a silly child and begged him not to go. "I don't want to lose you!" The words flew out of my mouth. I felt a full-fledged headache develop on the right side of my head and I had to go to bed. It's funny, right now I have a pounding headache.

H: You've been going through some intense feelings. What was your premonition?

M: I saw Sam falling asleep at the wheel and saw him crashing. Maybe these feelings are causing my pounding headache.

H: That headache may be a signal that there's something valuable pushing up from your unconscious. The fear you feel about Sam leaving is not rational. So when have you felt these feelings before?

M: (She drops her head, puts a hand on her forehead, and closes her eyes.)

Oh, my God! It's Charlie's crash!

(Her tears begin to flow . . . She starts in a low voice.)

It was dark, so dark. We were in the car and it was raining. I saw the other car coming straight for us. I knew somewhere deep inside that we didn't have time, we just didn't have time. I screamed Charlie's name and then everything went dark. After I came to, I rode with Charlie in the ambulance. His eyes were closed. I held his hand tight and I whispered in his ear that everything would be alright. I listened hard for his response. When he didn't answer, I raised my voice, pleading with him to answer, to say something. Fighting down the growing dread that he was dying, I got louder and louder. I must have panicked. I screamed to him to wake up, to open his eyes, not to be dead! There was so much I needed to say to him. I insisted he couldn't leave! I *had* to tell him my deep feelings for him . . . the ambulance attendant quieted me down. I remember feeling sick, chilled and hot at the same time. I didn't know if I was dreaming or if it was real. When we got to the hospital I was given a sedative. I don't remember much more than that, except that when I woke up, a doctor told me Charlie had died. (Sobbing pretty hard. A long pause before Molly looks up at Dr. Holman and continues.)

You know, Dr. Holman, my brother was a recovering alcoholic. He worked very hard for his recovery. Once he became sober at twenty one, he was happy and so proud of himself. He had realized he would be a dead man if he kept drinking like that. "A dead man." Those were his words.

We were hit head-on. God, a reformed alcoholic killed by a drunk driver.

H: It's ironic. And tragic.

M: I still feel outrage towards that driver. But I'm ashamed to say I also feel furious right now, thinking about Charlie not wearing his seatbelt. Why didn't I insist?

H: So you've carried this anger and fear for twenty-five years.

M: Yes, you're right. I see that I've never let Charlie go.

H: Why do you think you held onto these desperate, angry, painful feelings about Charlie for so long?

M: (Wailing) I don't know! For one thing, I didn't know I had them. Also, I may have been afraid to remember, to re-experience all that painful turmoil.

H: Better to let sleeping dogs lie? Perhaps both of your guesses are right. But you know, Molly, over the years I puzzled over this question of why we consciously hold onto our traumatic experiences. I finally came up with a good story about why we do it. Do you want to hear it?

M: Of course!

H: First, in each of us there is a spark of unquenchable optimism. It's like we never totally lose the hope that one day, somehow, we will find that "sweet moment" of unconditional, all embracing love that we know exists for us some where or when. Second, those of us who have a deep-seated belief that there is fairness and justice in the world also believe that if we have been made to suffer, justice will prevail, and that means we have hope that we will be rewarded fairly and fully.

(Molly seems calmer as she listens)

H: Many people are very reluctant to be mad at dead people, but now you can see how it has been affecting you. Even though you are very happy with Sam, you unconscious plays a different tune. You've carried all that old grief and anger from your resentment toward Charlie into you relationship with Sam.

M: You know, I felt so good after that Dome thing – could we try that with Charlie?

H: Sure.

M: First, I'll imagine a Safety Dome. Its walls are so strong that nothing I do or say will get through to the outside and no one outside will be hurt or even know about it.

Damn it Charlie! Why the hell didn't you wear your seatbelt? I hate that you left me behind. I hate that I didn't insist you put your seatbelt on . . . your stubbornness reminds me of Daddy.

H: That's right. Allow all your pent-up feelings to come out.

M: I am screaming, yelling, hitting, biting . . .

Dr. Holman reminds Molly not to forget her anger toward the drunk driver. He leads Molly through the Safety Dome where she expresses her rage at Charlie for not wearing his seat belt and for leaving her.

M: Now I feel as through Charlie really, really understands me, really hears me.

H: Would this be a good time to tell Charlie all the things you wanted to tell him in the ambulance?

M: Noooo! I would rather write to him in my journal.

H: That's fine. We can go on to the next part. So now have Charlie say, "Molly, I've caused you so much distress and trouble by dying and leaving you. Would you be willing to let me make it up to you?"

M: (to Dr. Holman) How can a dead person make it up to me?

H: By recognizing that you are talking to *your image* of Charlie. *Your image* is very much alive. And *your image* has just changed from someone who abandoned you to someone who is very much present in your Inner World – and who wants to fulfill your wishes – if you are willing to let him.

M: Am I willing? Well, yes, since he has heard me and understands me.

H: If he could, what would you want him to do to make it up to you?

M: I would want him to come back to life!

H: The inner world image of Charlie is alive in you. You have the power to access his image, his voice, his kind actions and the fun you shared.

M: (With her eyes closed) Yes, I can see his blue eyes looking at me with such love. He was so handsome. . . I can see his crooked smile, his long, light brown hair, like when we were having fun teasing each other. I can feel the sweetness of his love.

H: What else can you see?

M: (After a pause) I see him teaching me to ride his old two-wheeled bike after school, before my dad got home from work. My father had said I was too young to ride a bike. Charlie was also the one who taught me to roller skate, and how to drive. He even paid for the minor scrapes on my car so my parents wouldn't get mad at me and take away my driving privileges.

H: Molly? Do you feel made up to?

M: (Opens her eyes, smiling) I can't explain it, but I do.

H: Did you know you can bring back your good images and feelings about Charlie any time you like?

M: I see what you mean. I see now that I have a beautiful perception of Charlie available to me. I can embrace him, and I feel very loving towards him. (Molly paused) I'm seeing how it's possible I have projected all my fear and worry about the accident that killed Charlie onto Sam. I feel like it fits. You know, right now, I'm not afraid.

Journal #1 After Session #8

It's 9 P.M. I'm wide awake and grateful. My trust in Dr. Holman gave me the courage to let out my rage and yell at the drunk driver who killed my Charlie. I trust more and more that if I let out my anger, nothing bad will happen to me.

I can hardly believe that I've been storing so much anger all these years. I can't believe I could yell at a dead person, but I did! And damn, it felt good!

Today with Holman, I remembered Charlie's accident and death in a new and deeper way. I was able to express my buried rage at the drunk driver. I felt like an Amazon woman. It was as though I really did kill him, that drunk driver I've been carrying around in me, with my rage and my words.

Something huge has shifted. I'm amazed at how peaceful I feel. I wonder if this approach could help my relationship with my mother. I'll ask Dr. Holman. Even my feelings towards Mom have softened. I want to love her. She needs me now, more than ever. I can do this. I can love her, help her and be there with her.

I want to forgive her for burying her sadness in alcohol. It's only anger that keeps me from loving my mother. I've put up barriers to loving her because she couldn't handle Charlie's death the way I wanted her to. God forgive me.

Journal #2 After Session #8

Now that I'm in therapy, I'm beginning to look for hidden meaning to my upsets. I'm looking beneath the surface to find my buried treasures.

In the last few days I've gone from feeling justifiably angry when Sam fell asleep on the couch, and spoiled my wonderful fantasy evening, to deciding that I don't like the feeling of being angry with him. I sincerely want to stop playing the victim and I want to recognize what part I play in the demise of my own good feeling.

What I didn't know is that I can separate my thoughts from my feelings. That's huge. When I look at what I'm thinking, at the stories I've created that cause me to feel bad, I see that I can re-write the bad stories and make good ones! So now I can choose to focus on my good memories of Charlie instead of coming undone. Dr. Holman encourages me to stay with the good memories and feelings. He says, "Allow them to go deeper and deeper until you feel the pleasure you experienced earlier in your life."

I amaze myself! I took a giant step over a crevasse I had been afraid to cross. It felt dangerous, until I realized the crevasse was in my mind, not in the outer world. I gave myself permission to feel good about my brother's happy times instead of continuing to think I was being loyal to Charlie's memory. It feels great to know that I'm learning the process of getting to my happy memories and feelings.

Journal Before Session #9
Tuesday Evening

Thank God I'm home. I think this is the worst night of my life. I'm still in shock! To think Sam is an alcoholic and a secret one at that.

Tonight when I opened my lingerie drawer at Sam's, I found a couple of half-empty, pint sized liquor bottles among my sexy lingerie. In that moment, my body started pumping with fury and fear. My mind felt like an arrow poised to kill the target. I remember Sam's eyes were black as coal; I'm not sure if he was scared of me or trying to hold something back. My voice was low and hateful – I was damn sure those bottles were his, no matter how he denied it.

He chuckled off - handedly when I accused him of being an alcoholic. I needed to get away from him to think. I felt crippled by fear.

I didn't notice that it was raining and windy when I got into my car. It felt like the wind must have pushed me home. Through my tears, I could see the blur of the lights of oncoming traffic. My body felt like I'd been hurt in an accident. It was all a nightmare! A real nightmare, and I'd been here before.

What a liar! Sam said his father has a thing for me and hid the bottles among my sexy lingerie! How disgusting.

Imagine, two hours ago, I was reveling in my erotic fantasy. How carefree and high I felt from my fantasies as I was belting out "I've Got You Under My Skin," flying in my open silver convertible. I could have cared less that anybody could hear my sexy throaty voice.

Now all I want to do is put Sam, and his dad, in a boxing ring and knock them out cold. That will show them! And after the count of ten, I want them carried out on stretchers.

I love this feeling of strength and victory. I've just gone from fear to such excitement!

Do I want to make-up and forgive? Noooo -- but I'm not as angry as I was an hour ago. I feel like I'm spinning the Wheel of Fortune ---

spinning, spinning and I have no control over where it will land. I feel furious, but after I piled up my four pillows and beat them as if I were beating Sam (in my Inner World!) I felt better, but I'm still wondering if he'll ever talk to me again. Okay, I'll call, only I don't know what to say.

What a mistake! I should never have called. I'm a fool! And he's an idiot!

I told him I had never felt such rage before. I told him that I want to understand what happened, and that I feel awful. He just said, "Thank you for calling," and hung up.

I feel as if I.ve been struck by lightning. Oh, dear God. What if we're through?

I know I'll never sleep tonight. I have to call Dr. Holman's exchange and leave an emergency message. I just have to see him tomorrow.

Session #9
Two Vows – Wednesday Evening

M: Thank goodness you had an opening! I couldn't wait to finish work and see you.

H: What's happening?

M: I feel my whole world is falling apart. I think Sam's been keeping a huge secret from me and I think he may have lied to me.

H: Oh?

M: Last night I went over to Sam's house. While he was taking a shower, I decided to put on something sexy. When I opened the drawer where I keep my sexy lingerie, I discovered two half-full bottles of scotch. At that moment, Sam came out of the shower. When I confronted him, he told me his father hides bottles of scotch around his house, and then he laughed! I just knew he was lying.

    I raged at him. I couldn't help it. It just came out--full and overflowing, like Vesuvius. I know alcoholics, I know what they do. They hide bottles. They keep secrets and if they're caught they try to laugh it off. I know alcoholics deny things. They don't even admit to themselves that they could possibly be an alcoholic.

    I kept thinking about my father. It was years before I understood how he kept his alcoholic behavior a secret. He would always drink with his buddies at the club.

H: *(nods)*

M: Has Sam been keeping the same secret? How could I be so stupid? I can't believe I've spent months with this man! It's horrifying to think I might be destined to live with an alcoholic my whole life. How could I ever trust a man who kept such a secret? I thought we were soul mates. This is the man I vowed to spend the rest of my life with, and he turns out to be a closet alcoholic! (Starts to cry) What am I going to do?

H: This has stirred up a lot. What are you thinking of?

M: (Through tears) Well, you know I vowed never to marry an alcoholic after what I went through with my mother and father.

H: What led you to make the vow?

M: I couldn't reach either of my parents – everything was hidden. The worst is that I felt they didn't love me. (Tears start again) I felt desperate and helpless to do anything about it.

H: Is that why you made your vow?

M: Yes. I vowed I would never marry an alcoholic. I wouldn't want to be married to a man whose personality is veiled by alcohol. It feels like you can't reach an alcoholic, that no one is at home. I didn't want a man who would repeat what my parents did. I don't want to go through that ever again.

H: That was a big decision. Having made the vow, how did you feel?

M: I felt strong and powerful. I knew if I got involved with a man who turned out to be an alcoholic, I would know just what to do, I would be prepared. I would break it off immediately.

So then, when I saw those bottles in the drawer, the picture of my mother and my pain around her drinking came back to me. It was such a shock! I was trembling inside and out and it was hard to breathe. I felt I had to break up with Sam, that I had to be strong and carry out my vow.

I just couldn't let myself be married to an alcoholic. (Crying) But I love Sam. Do you understand, Dr. Holman, I committed to marry this man?

H: Do you know the word "beshert"? It means "meant to be."

M: Okay, Sam and I are "beshert." When I'm with him every cell in my body comes alive. No matter what I'm doing when I think of him, I feel good. When he's around, it feels like springtime. This is the man I've been waiting for all my life. He's my soul mate, and now I have to give him up?

H: I understand why you feel so torn. You've found your soul mate that you vowed to marry, and now you've remembered your vow never to marry an alcoholic. You're caught between two vows you made in childhood.

M: What do you mean by vows I made in childhood?

H: We forget we made these vows in childhood and that they become guiding beliefs by which we live; we don't even remember we made them. These old beliefs, the child's vows, come up in times of crisis. But these commitments are challenged by the realities of today.

M: What do you mean?

H: Let's address your vow to marry your soul mate. "Soul   mate" is your child's concept. I think for you it includes total honesty, total understanding and total unconditional love coming from your perfect man. He is everything you want. So it's understandable why you would want to fulfill your vow to be with him forever.

M: What am I supposed to do?

H: What comes into your mind?

M: If only I knew for sure the bottles were his father's . . . but I have a gut feeling that they're Sam's. I *know* they're Sam's.

H: Tell me about your gut feeling.

M: When I have gut feelings . . . well, I trust my gut feelings. If there's anything I trust, it's my gut feelings.

H: So your gut feelings make you feel sure you know to whom the bottles belong?

M: Yes, they couldn't be his father's bottles . . . but then again, his father does come over a lot to putter around the garage.

H: I'm thinking about how anger can influence gut feelings, throw us off track sometimes. It's hard to put your full trust in your gut feeling.

M: You mean I can't trust my gut feelings if I'm angry?

H: It sounds like your justified anger created a bad story in your gut and you believed it.

M: But the proof was in the drawer! It's not just a story.

H: Yes, it's true, you   did   have   evidence.   But   then,   do   you actually know to whom the bottles belong?

M: No. (A puzzled look comes on her face.) I forgot that I really don't know.

H: Could your anger relate to anything in the past or does it feel as if it's in the present?

M: Well, it seems   obvious to me   now.   I remember   my *mother* also hid bottles. Honestly it makes me feel as though I'm going to throw up. So you're saying that all the anger I felt about my mother's drinking, that I never expressed as a child, came out last night directed at Sam? And at myself too? That's the worst part – I sacrificed my relationship with Sam.

I sure feel justified being so angry . . . maybe that's why I feel so sure they're *his* bottles.

H: The unfinished anger from the past often manifests as justified anger in the present.

By the way, it's odd, isn't it, that your mother and Sam both drink scotch and hide bottles?

M: What? Oh my God! Oh my God! (shrieks) Sam doesn't even drink scotch! He only drinks vodka!

Journal #1 After Session #9
Wednesday Night

There is so much I need to tell Sam, but I'm afraid to pick up the phone. I have to tell him about my extraordinary session with Dr. Holman when I found out what an idiot I was last night.

I feel so terribly sorry that I yelled at you, for accusing you of something that was not true. I do not believe that you are an alcoholic.

I hope Sam will be open to hear me and believe how sorry I am. It must have been shocking for him, seeing me turn into an alien within seconds. I want to understand where the alien came from so that will never happen again. In the moment, it's not easy for me to recognize the influence of the old, buried, negative stuff – and it's impact on my life today.

It may be hard for you to believe, Sam, but I treasure you!

Will he ever be willing to forgive me for not believing him?

I choose to imagine that Sam will be glad I called him and he'll reassure me that he loves me. That thought feels much better. I'll call quickly before I lose this good feeling.

Journal #2 After Session #9
Thursday Morning

This morning the doorbell rang at seven a.m. and there was Sam standing at the door smiling, handing me a latte. I had cried all night thinking Sam never wanted to see me again. I went to the door without a thought about my puffy eyes, still crying because I thought I had lost Sam forever. I was so relieved and thrilled to see him. I threw my arms around him and gave him the biggest kiss. He put the coffee down and kissed my red, swollen face all over. Holding me tight, he said, "Oh my sweet, Molly, I loved your message and I love you."

Today I'm full of love. Yesterday I was distraught, thinking that Sam was a secret alcoholic. Where did all my justified anger go? Where did all the love go?

I pretended this whole drama, and then I projected my rage at him!! I feel terrible that I blamed and accused my beloved, innocent Sam.

I think I slipped Mom's image into Sam's place without even being aware of it myself. I'm recognizing how I did this blame game with Mom too. I can't go on blaming my mother for everything. I used to say Mom put up walls between us. If I'm feeling walled off, are these walls my mother's or mine?

Journal Before Session #10

I see how angry I was with my mother throughout my childhood. I hated how she hid from me when she came home, so I wouldn't see she had been drinking. I hated eating alone or in the kitchen with the maid, when she was upstairs alone too. I hated knowing she wasn't eating dinner again. I hated hearing her cry behind the bedroom door and I hated being afraid to go in and comfort her.

I remember hearing my parents having loud discussions when my father came home late. When I came into the room, they stopped. Then my mother locked herself in the bathroom.

I hate that in high school I started drinking wine. I hate that I spent so many hours in sexual fantasies instead of doing my homework. I thought my stories were good enough to publish in an underground press, but I was afraid to show them to anyone.

At dinner one night, my mom spilled her water. I wanted to yell, "You're drunk!" but I wanted to protect my dad. I didn't know if he knew that Mom was drunk. Thinking back, I realize we all had secrets.

Session #10

M: Last night I had another one of my sleepless nights. I feel horrible that I treated Sam as an enemy -- as a betrayer. I showed no trust in him and I didn't even give him a chance to talk. I was the judge and jury. The verdict was in.

H: Are you aware that you're still angry now?

M: Yes, I am angry. I felt justified for attacking myself these past two days. I felt horrible for being so mean to Sam when he had nothing to do with it.

H: What stirred these upset feelings that seemed to consume you?

M: When I found the bottles in the drawer, I couldn't see straight. I didn't even see it was scotch, not vodka because it brought up so many negative feelings. The worst was that it brought me back to my childhood when I felt angry and helpless.

I remember one day I had my best friend over and we were looking through an old trunk where my mom kept her mother's old, fancy clothes. As we dug down I found a half-empty bottle of Grant's scotch. We both laughed, but I knew that my mother had hidden the bottle. I had come across many secret bottles all over the house.

The sad thing is, I was afraid my mother's drunken behavior meant there was something terribly the matter with me – the way she avoided me, the way she refrained from talking to me. I believed these things meant she didn't want to be with me because she didn't like me.

H: You knew your mother had a big problem.

M: Yes, but I didn't identify it as alcoholism. I didn't know what that was. I thought it had something to do with me. I vowed I would never keep secrets from the people I love.

H: You really felt shut out from your mother.

M: Yes, I was very angry. It felt like I didn't have a real mother.

H: If you could go back as that little girl, what would you like to say to her?

M: I don't know. I haven't thought about it.

H: If you put your image of your mother in this other chair and pretend to talk to her, do you think you could express some of your anger?

M: I don't think so.

H: Are you afraid?

M: Yes. (pause) Mom, I'm afraid. I'm afraid you're sick and may be dying. I'm scared that you drink too much. I hate that you hide from me. I hate that I have to hide my friends from you. I hate when you and Daddy come home from parties. I run into your room late wanting to hear about the party and you send me back to my room. The rest of the world gets the beautiful mother and I get the unavailable drunken mother. Your love for alcohol seems bigger than your love for me. I need you and I can't count on you. Sometimes I can reach you; when I can't, I feel very angry, and then I hate you. I can't trust you. (Molly starts to cry.) I love you and you broke my heart.

Journal #1 after Session #10
1st Two-chair Dialogue

One of the most amazing parts of my last session came during a two-chair dialogue when I sat with my inner world mother. She acknowledged my years of childhood pain. My mother began to cry. She said that I was right, and how terribly sorry she was for not being the mother I wanted.

The best part was when she asked me if there was any way she could make it up to me. At first I couldn't think of a way. Through her tears, she added, "If I could make it up to you, would you let me?"

I thought about it. Could I let go of my anger? Did I really want friendship with my mother? I'm the creator of what I want. I can create a new version of my mother. I knew that now. I'd learned it. I believe that it is true. I also realized if I said "No," I was going to be hurting myself. I said, "Yes."

She followed up with, "How?"

I finally decided to ask her to do some very specific things I missed as a child. She said, "My darling, Molly. I'm more than willing to do them."

"Stop drinking! Go to AA meetings. Go to a good therapist. Take responsibility and be a real mom. Be persistent and follow through."

After I took the time to have her do everything I asked, I felt loved by her. To my surprise, I felt full of appreciation as I visualized her happily doing everything I asked her to do. When it came to the part about forgiving her, I was so full of good feelings that I freely forgave her. Our pretend embrace felt so real. After all these years of tension and hatred in my body and my head and my heart, I felt only love. It was a most wonderful and joyful sensation.

Now that I've found my treasure with my mom, I can see her life differently. I'm writing through tears, realizing how much I love my mother. When I think of what her disappointments in life have been, I can understand her drinking.

In some ways I can understand my dad's drinking too. He loved a good time. No wonder everybody called him "Good Time Charlie." He worked hard and got to be a VIP at the brewery. My parents tried to give me what they hadn't had as kids. I went to the best private schools and graduated from Brown. I was well prepared to walk into my job at the magazine and move up to Senior Editor.

Poor Mom. I can't imagine growing up in a large Irish family of ten kids in Boston. Thank God for my sweet grandma who picked my mom out of the ten as the most needy and gave her some T.L.C.

I have observed how my mother and Sara love each other easily. She has been a darling grandmother to her. I'm going to suggest we have a "peace talk" so I can begin to live each day knowing I am loved by her and she by me. I know it's late tonight, but I'm going to call her now and invite her to have lunch at the new Garden Café in Brentwood.

We have a lot of healing to do. What I want now is a chance to thank my mother for all she has given me.

Journal #2 after Session #10
2nd Two-chair Dialogue

Today in Holman's office I did another "two-chair dialogue" with my mother because I was remembering my 16th birthday. I wanted to do the exercise because the other time had been so successful, and I wanted to get rid of even more anger. So I was fearless and, boy, did I get mad! I really let her have it, more so than last time. As a child, I'd wanted to yell at her, grab her shoulders and shake her with all my might. But I always chickened out. Today I didn't pull any punches. I roared . . . and my "pretend" mother listened.

I got into her head and her heart so she could hear her daughter, me, cry and scream and blame her for making me suffer.

Does this sound crazy? I became my mother, with her sensibilities and her history and her slant on life -- not mine. And "my mother" heard me, so much so that she agreed once again that I had good reason to be mad, and she felt very sorry to have hurt me so. She asked if I would be willing to let her make it up to me. Holman reminded me that she was *my* image, and as such, she could do, and would willingly do whatever I wanted her to do. I threw the ball of responsibility in her court. "What would you like to do, Mom?" She thought for a minute and said, "Let's re-do your sixteenth birthday when I got so drunk and embarrassed you in front of your friends." And off she (we) went re-constructing the most wonderful birthday of my life . . . and it has stuck in my mind as the birthday I choose to remember. That birthday, my sixteenth, is now forever transformed. Resentment that I'd been harboring way too long, melted away. With the taste of sweet forgiveness in my mouth, I kissed and hugged my imaginary mother and felt more loving energy flow through my body. I whispered "thank you" to a smiling Dr. Holman.

Later when I told Sam about my session, he put on his silly grin and said, "You did ALL THAT in your head?"

In Place of Session #11
Journal #1
Molly Tells Same about Alcoholic Parents

I finally made a little bit of peace with Mom in Dr. Holman's office. I felt real forgiveness and I must say, genuine love and acceptance. I could see all her very real problems for the first time.

I feel more powerful today. I told Sam the secret of my alcoholic parents. It seemed less threatening today. Was that because I'm lighter or stronger? Bigger or smaller?

I chose a dark, cozy bar with a fireplace and soft couches that would set the stage for my story.

I cozied up to Sam and told him some back-story about my mother. I wanted him to like her. After all, she is kind of a lost soul. After Charlie died, both my parents were desolate. Dad had his priests, his cronies and his bars, but Mom had no one, not even me—and so she turned to her old friend, William Grant, purveyor of scotch for a deeper friendship. I lost both my parents.

I told Sam straight away that my parents were alcoholics. My face flushed and tears welled up. I hate secrets! And yet I kept the grand daddy of them all from my sweet love, since who my parents are is a big part of who I am. I kept that part of myself from Sam.

I'm glad I told him, but it was not easy at first. I hadn't wanted to tell him because I was sure he would be critical of me, especially since I had been so accusatory toward him and his father. He listened sympathetically and openly. Sam appreciated my honesty.

We joked about how I would stop projecting the negative feelings I felt for my mother onto him. He pretended to heave a sigh of relief and to wipe the worry-sweat from his brow. We fell into silly laughter, the sort that when one of us would begin to stop, the sight or sound of the other would start us up again and off we would go, laughing our heads off. I just love it when we laugh together like that. It feels like we are each so happy and free of ourselves that we expand and blend. I like feeling so connected.

As I write this I now understand that my therapy with Dr. Holman is giving me a chance to start over.

In Place of Session #11
Journal #2
Mom, Sam, Molly Journal

At dinner tonight with Sam, I talked more about my mother. I told him that Sara has a really close relationship with her. And for that matter, so does my former husband, Andy.

When I was growing up, my mother was not an abusive person, not a bad person; she was just not there. She was not available to me. When I think about it, Andy wasn't available to me, either. You, Sam, are different. I feel you are involved with me, and I am involved with you. You are responsive to my moods whether I speak them or not. You cherish me and I adore you.

I've often thought, "Why couldn't I have a relationship with my mother like Sara had?" Sara loves to spend days and nights with her. They laugh and giggle together. Mother seems very present. Sometimes she teases, but never angry. I've watched Sara cuddle up in Mother's arms ever since she was a baby. Now they watch TV together, Sara practically in Mother's lap. Oddly enough, Mother does not drink when Sara is visiting. To tell the truth, that really pisses me off. It isn't that I'm not happy for Sara, but why couldn't she have been that way with me?

Sam understood because his dad was the same as my mother. He could always tell when his father had been drinking. Sam's dad was closer to his dog than he was to Sam. We had a strange, dark bit of humor over that one!

I also shared with Sam some of my progress in therapy. I found out that I had learned how to do anger just the way Mother did. When things didn't go her way, she withdrew and took away her good feelings. I'm discovering her way doesn't work for me, so I'm trying something new.

Sam wanted to know what that new way would be. When I have a wish, the new way would be to talk to her about it. Instead of clamming up, I would tell her what I was thinking and feeling. Even if we didn't agree, at least we would know where we stood. Then it's nice to think we might discuss or negotiate.

I told Sam how Dr. Holman helped me to understand that when I blame someone else, I give away my power to make things better. Instead, I can keep my power by telling Mom how I want it to be.

Recently I've made an effort to ask for what I want. We went to church together, which we both enjoyed. I took her to the symphony at the Dorothy Chandler Pavilion and she really loved that. Even though things are better now than before, I've hesitated to tell Mom my big news . . . that I've found my soul mate. I know she adores Andy and my fear has been that Mom won't be enthusiastic towards Sam.

You know that old idea that children should be seen and not heard? Well, I'm shifting how I think about myself from being that little child to being a grown-up who has my own thoughts and feelings. I have a voice and a vote. This isn't feminism, I told Sam, its grown-up-ism.

In Place of Session #11
Journal #3
Sam and Mom Can Meet

I feel confident, now, that Sam and Mom can meet. I think he can handle her "differences" and her strange ways of seeing and being in this world. Sam knows what it's like to be around problem drinkers and he reassured me that together we can do this!

I made a bold call to Mom *after* six P.M., something I *never* do. And she wasn't too bad, really. I told her that I'd met the man of my dreams. She was characteristically mono-syllabic, but clearly interested. "Your 'soul mate'?" she repeated, as only she can. She is the perfect incarnation of my "critics committee." I imagine her words, "Molly, dear, surely you don't still believe in such childish fantasies?" But I, the grown-up Molly, didn't rise to the bait. Wait a minute! I didn't rise to my *own* bait! I'm the one who made up this sub-text of our story.

Anyway, she went along and actually scheduled lunch with Sam and me so they could meet. I am so excited and so afraid. Will she show up drunk? I made the time pretty early, 11:30 A.M. Will Sam connect with her, as he is so capable of doing with other people? Or will he be intimidated by her imperious aspect? She gets this look, especially after a few drinks, that would command respect if she were sober, but when drunk she looks comical and foolish to the world. I hate it when her nose is in the air and she looks *down* towards *me*!

Oh well, what the hell!!! Why am I worrying so much? There is no earthly benefit to worrying about it. Dr. Holman explains that worry is a story that takes place in the future, with a bad outcome to the self. He also says, "Fear is anger turned in." So if I don't futurize, I can go with "The Great I Don't Know."

Journal #1 in Place of Session #12
Mother Goes to Hospital

I was feeling happy when I called Mother to tell her Sam could make it. I had to leave a message on her answering machine.

I waited and waited for her return call. Then I left another message, "Mom, I really want to hear from you. Please call Saturday morning. I'll be home."

Did she call? No! By this time my enthusiasm was beginning to cool. I felt she was not interested in my doings. I also felt a little miffed. Couldn't she find a minute to pick up the phone? I began to think maybe she was in one of her moods and was isolating herself.

I felt irritated. Ignored. Cut off. I don't like feeling cut off. In the past, I would withdraw in cold anger. What I've learned in therapy is to take more active steps to get what I want, and to keep trying, not to stop after one attempt. So I called her again. Again, no answer. Then I was beginning to worry. Maybe she's been drinking too much. Maybe she passed out.

I started to feel mad. I could feel the old anger rising. Then I worried that something bad had happened to her. Then I realized these were *my* "stories". The fact is, I didn't really know what was happening with Mom.

I decided to take action. I went to her house. She didn't answer, but I was certain she was there. I knocked and yelled for several minutes. Finally, I went to the back of the house. The bathroom window was open, so I was able to look in. There was Mom, sprawled on the tile, her head bleeding from hitting the floor. I practically jumped through the window. She had passed out. I called 911, and then Sara. I asked her to go spend the night with the neighbors while I go to the hospital with Mom. I assured her that everything would be okay and I would see her tomorrow.

I was in need of a little support myself, so I called to tell Sam what happened to Mom. He wanted to rush over to help me, but I said no; I didn't want him to meet Mom in this condition.

I rode with her in the ambulance. She was out cold and pale as chalk. From the emergency room, she was admitted to the hospital for testing and observation.

Journal #2 in Place of Session #12
After I Took Mom to the Hospital

I hated to leave Mom alone in the hospital. Her thin lips were quivering when I told her that I wanted to pick up Sara from school and we would be right back. She held on to my hand and my arm and her amber eyes looked deep into my amber eyes.

I could see deep into the fears she had been trying to hide from me.

When I looked away, I felt my shield melt away. Our protection disappeared and we were two girls looking for a strong, protective mother.

I had no idea what she was going to go through. I know that I will be there for her and even though this sounded like a foreign language, I could say to Mom, "You may not know it, but I do love you." When I told her I could see I had been a rebellious child and that phase was gone forever, she started to sob. This is so hard to write without feeling like an idiot – a voice in my head is saying, "Isn't this a little late?" I agree with that voice and I do feel miserable. Yet, I also have a small voice telling me what I learned from the book Tuesdays with Morrie. The author, while a graduate student, treated his professor, Morrie, with disdain. Years later, he recognized the wonderful qualities of his mentor, his love and interest. He sought him out, only to find him dying. He visited Morrie every Tuesday – establishing a deep bond of admiration and love for the dying man. It gave me inspiration to reclaim my long buried love for my mom.

Tonight Sara told me that she had called her Dad and that he wanted to come down from Montana to be here for her, Mom, and me.

It's 11:00 in the evening. After calling to make arrangements with Andy, I had a good cry. I need him now. I can't believe I can say that after five years of feeling righteously angry with him.

Mom truly loves Andy almost as much as she loved the son she lost. I am grateful to my Sara for asking Andy to help us. Mostly, I can't believe the change in my heart – it's full of love.

Journal #3 in Place of Session #12
Diagnosis and Prognosis

When I saw Andy walk into the hospital room today, I opened my arms, and when he put his arms around me, I stated to cry – so much has happened. Sara wondered what the tears were about. Earlier, I had reassured her that Grandma was going to be okay. Now, with Andy's help, I was able to tell her that we didn't know how sick Grandma actually was and we didn't have all the information yet from the x-rays and tests.

At that moment, the doctor came in to see how my mother was doing and asked Andy and me to meet him in the waiting room.

Because our family had been seeing him for many years, when he came in, I could tell something was very serious. I reached for Andy's hand as he told us that it was cirrhosis of the liver and that most of the liver was already damaged. She didn't have much time.

When the doctor left us, I felt cold and began to shiver. Andy started to cry. My mind was flooded with memories of all the times I was mad at my mother. Now I had been planning a happier new chapter in our relationship, similar to what Sara had with Mother. Was I losing my chance to start over?

Andy told me how much he hated living so far from my mother and how much he missed their relationship.

When we walked back into the room, Sara was lying on the hospital bed next to mother with her arm across her chest, patting mother's shoulder.

After they changed the IV, we said goodbye. I hated leaving her alone, but the nurse said she would pay special attention.

At home, Andy and I were making a little dinner but we were still in shock. It seemed hard to find a way to tell Sara.

Sara looked at our faces and asked, "What's going on? What did the doctor say, that he couldn't say in front of Grandma and me?"

I said to Sara, "she doesn't have long to live." Sara ran to Andy and he tried to comfort her. Sara asked, sobbing, "It has to do with her drinking, doesn't it?"

Between sobs, she told us how she had tried to get her grandmother to stop drinking and she had failed. I told her it was a long story that started when I was a little girl.

"Why didn't Grandpa do something about it?" Sara asked angrily.

I explained that he tried, to no avail. "It seemed she was determined to destroy herself."

Andy told us, "I have a terrible headache." Sara said, "Poor Daddy. Poor Daddy." She took out the ibuprofen and tried to comfort him. She lay down beside her dad on her bed and before we knew it, she was asleep.

As we moved into the living room, Andy broke down. I gave him a damp cool towel for his head. I went to the liquor cabinet and poured us shots of scotch. "I haven't had hard liquor since I started therapy, I told him as we touched glasses. "I'm so glad you're here with me. It feels like we used to feel when things were good between us. I can see you're in no shape to be alone; would you like to stay over tonight?" Andy's answer was a big hug.

Journal #4 in Place of Session #12
Molly's Jealousies

As the days passed, I was sitting in my usual chair in Mom's hospital room watching Andy combing Mother's thick, white hair and putting a bow in her hair. She means so much to him. She was the "Good Mother" he found when he married me. He really treasures her.

I try to pretend that I don't care how close Mom and Andy are, and how they enjoy each other. If I pretend I don't care, I'm afraid Andy will see through me after all these years. I am embarrassed to be caught sulking and I'm ashamed of being jealous of a dying woman's relationship with a man she loves like a son. Of course Mom and Dad wanted a son to replace Charlie, but I was the one and only until Andy came along.

I remember when I was four. I was number one with mother. We would do all these things together until Charlie was born. It felt like mother stopped liking me and only liked Charlie. I couldn't see why she did it. Maybe I had been a bad girl or done something wrong. I wanted to be the one who romps with her, but I felt I couldn't. Now I can see that I was jealous, then and now again as I see her and Andy together. And I'm jealous of Sara, my own daughter! Mother never seems to treat Sara with the indifference she showed me as a child.

I saw Sara reading her a piece she wrote in school about her wonderful Grandmother. Mom smiled and looked so lovingly at Sara. I so want to be part of it too, but I found myself held back in my chair.

I felt the green-eyed monster rising up inside me. I hate this feeling! I want to be the one doing these things with mom. I am jealous of Sara!

I hate it that I have such childish feelings! When Andy and Sara and I were walking to the hospital elevator from Mom's room, Andy asked me what was the matter. I couldn't admit to my jealousy. When we were married, Andy hated my jealousy. So I lied. Not exactly a lie, because I believed it. I told him my heart was broken over Mom's imminent death and that I wasn't ready. I never got a chance to heal my feelings of hurt and rejection with her, and now it's too late.

When we got home, and Sara had gone next door to her friend's house, Andy looked at me and asked, "Did you tell me the real reason you were upset in the hospital?"

"Do you think I was lying to you?"

Andy wasn't fooled by my ploy. "Well, were you?"

He knows one of my buttons is being called a liar. "You know all my life I hated being called a liar!" I felt justified to blame him for my painful feelings. "A liar is a terrible thing to call me."

Just last night I told him how deeply touched I was by his relationship with my mother. I told him how much he means to me. And now, twenty-four hours later, I am jealous and angry with him. No wonder he looked like he'd been attacked again by the green-eyed monster.

I hope Andy doesn't see my therapy as a failure since I am still reacting to this same old button. Why do I have to feel jealous? Why do I have to put my blame on Andy? I guess this huge anger is what Holman calls Reservoir Anger. How am I going to stop this jealousy, anger and my shame about it?

At least I was able to tell Andy afterward that this was not about him. I owned that it was really about me. I wanted him to know that I was trying to handle my feelings in a more adult manner. I can understand, though, why he said, "Thank goodness I'm staying at your mother's. This is too much for me. You know how I feel when I get blamed for nothing."

I tried to hug him and tell him I was so sorry, and repeated that it was not about him. It was my anger. He was determined to leave. I yelled after him, "Don't give up on me!"

He didn't look back. He just nodded.

Journal #5
Session #12
Swimming Pool – Fantasy with Andy

I had lots on my mind when I went for my session today. I blurted out to Dr. Holman that I'd been having sexual fantasies about Andy. I felt my face flush and my neck beamed red. Dr. Holman said, "Yes, go on."

I asked Dr. Holman if I'd mentioned the day I found Andy sunbathing by Mom's pool. I described what really happened as a "fantasy" because I was too embarrassed to tell Holman the truth.

I had teased Andy and said, "You're lucky you're wearing your swim trunks." When he got up from the chaise to kiss me, he caught me off-guard and I slipped, tripping him into the pool. I jumped in after him and gave him the longest, and surely the wettest kiss underwater. When we burst up from the bottom, he drew me to him and kissed me back. I pulled down his trunks, and we both took off my blouse and skirt while he kissed as many parts of me as he could get his mouth on. He is titillated (pun intended) by my secret: no panties. With that, he pulls me underwater, and amid the bubbles, he mouths "I want you." I let him make love to me, four different ways.

We collapsed on the blanket and he continued kissing me, whispering, "I adore you."

I watched Dr. Holman carefully as I told him my fantasy, hoping to get a reading on what he was thinking. I loved his interest. I wonder if he has sexual fantasies too. Dare I ask? Wouldn't it be fun if he had them about me!

Journal #6 Session #12
Topanga Beach with Andy

It was a beautiful day as Andy and I left home to take Sara to school. The temperature was close to eighty. I called the doctor, who said mother was holding her own. I called the magazine to tell them I wouldn't be in. Andy and I took off for the Beach where we lived in a wooden cottage before Sara was born.

The sand was hot, the heat sexy. Lying in the sun, barely clothed, often makes me feel sexy, even when I'm alone. But beside me was Andy, my beloved first and only husband, my friend, and the father of sweet Sara.

Of course his very presence, plus the smell of sun and ocean, brought back memories. How could it not? As we lay quietly, my mind sped back to times before we were married. I was awakened when he rolled over and kissed me. He stood there a minute reciting his old "one, two, three" before he made a brave running dive into the whitewater, at once fearless and afraid. When I saw his shoulders disappear, I was reminded of Malibu when and where we fell in love . . .

His shoulders, were brown and straight; so broad, so able to bear anything, built strong by ten years of surfing and volleyball. We felt like we were "the king and queen" of the beach in those days, those Topanga Beach days. We walked the same stretch of beach together up and back, two, three times a day – laughing, loving, looking, but our favorite I think was being looked-at. All of them (boys and girls alike) watched him; some of them watched me. But we were, as individuals and as a couple, impenetrable, just out of reach, and like all youth, infallible, omnipotent and beautiful.

With eyes closed, I was off in this dream of years past. With that vital heat on my stomach inspiring surprising lust for Andy, I sensed his presence at the foot of my towel. I hadn't heard him, hadn't seen him. He wasn't dripping water, not making any sound. Yet I sensed he was there, felt him there, opened my eyes to see the four o'clock sun turn him into a silhouette, a haloed god. Only the dark outline of his wet curls and those shoulders met my squinting eyes. He said nothing. To this day, I'm still amazed at how he can say nothing yet communicate so loudly. His eyes clearly spoke to me, and mine, as clearly, responded.

Lying in the sand beside me, he spoke my name softly. I opened my eyes. I would feel the pleasure of my interrupted dream flowing out toward him in an embracing smile. He smiled back, leaned over and kissed me – a forever kiss.

I stood up, leaving books and beach chairs behind, and we walked slowly toward our palapa.

Journal #7 Session #12
Conversation with Kay re: Andy and Sam

After what happened with Andy, I was riding on a high! I felt nostalgia for the good times we had together, so I put on a stack of Frank Sinatra CD's. When Frank sang "Bewitched, Bothered and Bewildered," I dialed my best friend Kay, to confess these newfound sexy feelings for Andy.

I knew Kay would not judge me. I began talking low and softly as if I were a schoolgirl talking to a priest in the confessional box – sexy secrets! So deceptively thrilling! At first Kay listened just like the priest, unseen but her godlike presence felt. Then she became excited, probably secretly hoping this was a good sign that I would return to Andy and re-unite the family. Kay knew and loved Andy the 10 years we were married, and although she liked Sam and could see why I fell in love with him, still I think she's rooting for Andy.

Finally Kay said, "Molly, you never cease to amaze me. You're my kaleidoscope."

A part of me wanted Kay to give me a little advice, the kind that would resolve my confusion and calm me down. Even though I knew advice would not really help, Kay's words did make a difference. I love Kay's faith in me.

Session #13 Journal #1
Hospital / Molly and Andy go out for an Ice Cream Cone

Dear, dear Andy, keeping vigil with me at the hospital, spelling me, even holding my hand. This morning he popped in with a shocking magenta sunrise cactus plant and an optimistic smile and hug for Mom. He whispered an invitation to me to partake in a large waffle cone of mocha almond fudge. I swear, the man is inspired!

As we walked toward the elevator, he put his arm around me as if I were still his wife, still his and asked, "I'm willing to make amends. Are you?"

Ordering ice cream cones dipped in peanuts and "jimmies," his gluttonous triple scoop and my disciplined and saintly single, this process was lovingly familiar and it felt so good, so right. Too good! Too right!

We walked along the Palisades, a welcome breath of sea air after hours in the hospital. Both of us looking towards the gray pacific, Andy said, "I like you. I like this new you. You seem less angry, softer, more open. I watched with pleasure as you spoke to Sara and comforted your mom. You don't seem as afraid or guarded. Where's your armor, Molly? What have you done with the "unsinkable Molly Brown?"

I loved listening to him carefully choose his words. He was really puzzled and seemed really pleased. And since his curiosity was genuine, I responded in kind. I tried to take Holman's innovative philosophy and make it not only clear but palatable. Andy can be such a cynic.

Holman's "reservoir" is key to understanding what's been going on within me, but sometimes it's difficult to explain. I began with, "I have a new talent: I can choose to empty negative, judgmental or ugly stuff out of my heart or out of my reservoir (think of a trash can filled with minute monsters from your past who are trying to get out and attack everyone who ever criticized you or made you feel unworthy or bad). But I am really afraid that bad things will happen to me if I lift the lid and allow my saved-up anger to spew out. So I am learning how to let all this angry stuff out without hurting anyone – or myself.

I want to get free of blaming; I want to feel loving and forgiving of myself and everyone around me.

The thought of love and forgiveness made me well up. Andy knew instantly what the tears and unspoken words meant...

He said "I'm willing to take on as much responsibility as you would like to give me."

God, he knows her as well, maybe better, than I do! Surrounded by my fear about her death and my sweet little blue-eyed mother's fear of dying, we are held and comforted by Andy, my former husband, her son-in-law.

Session #13 Journal #2
Molly Asks Sam to Wait

I'm having love feelings for Andy and I'm "in love" with Sam!

This afternoon Sam came in the house to pick me up just as Andy and Sara were leaving for the movies. Waiting until the coast was clear, I jumped on Sam's lap, saying how much I'd missed kissing him and teasing him, and (I whispered in his ear) fucking his ridiculously beautiful body. He stood up, putting me on my feet singing, "Well, here I am, baby!" Taking me by the hand, we danced all the way to the bed.

I couldn't do it.

"I need to ask you for a favor, Sweet Sam. I need some time and space to be with my mother, to focus on her since we're just beginning to understand each other." I tried to explain myself again and after three sentences, he cut me off.

"Okay, Molly. I don't like being out of the picture, but if that's what you need . . ." And from there he became Sam the gracious, Sam the gentleman, Sam the Sweet.

Back at the hospital, I felt surprised by my overwhelming feelings for Andy. Sara, Andy and I seem like a family; in fact we are a family when we're around Mom's bedside.

Mom, my pretty little mother, so small beneath those sheets – I feel closer than ever just as death threatens to separate us. In death I feel our love will survive but in life our love was complicated by anger. She needs my focus, it's true, and I want to give it to her.

My heart is big – it feels expansive and forgiving. There's room for everyone in my heart, but with Andy back on the scene it's a little crowded in the outside world. It hurts me not to tell Sam the whole truth right now, that I need time to sort out my feelings for Andy. The greatest thing will be the loss of my first love, my mother.

Session #13 Journal #3
Sara Feels Left Out (re: Andy)

I remember the way Mom looked into Dad's eyes and they both smiled as if they had a secret between them. I never felt part of their marriage bond, so I vowed my child would always feel included. Andy loved Sara so much and was delighted to have her join us in our bed until she was about six. We had such fun playing and laughing together, no wonder Sara was broken-hearted when we separated. When Andy left, she blamed me. Now that he's back in town, I feel old loving feelings stirring in both of us.

Recently when Sara caught Andy and I giving each other secret looks, I sensed she felt left out, just as I did at her age.

I have to sit down and talk heart-to-heart with Sara. That scares me. For five years she's thought she had Andy to herself. Now she sees Andy and I together, so I'm the interloper, again.

Session #13 Journal #4
Chasing the Blues Away

About 9 am this morning I was sitting alone in the waiting room feeling very blue. Mom was being fussed over by her exceptional nurses so I told Mom I was going down to the cafeteria for breakfast, but I couldn't eat. The food wouldn't go down over the lumps of sadness in my throat.

Sweet Andy came into the waiting room whistling and when he saw me hunched over he pulled me up and gave me a long tender hug. I felt warmed and comforted.

Then he began singing a song from the 30's called "Sunny Side of the Street." Like a song and dance man he sang,

"Grab your coat and get your hat
Leave your worries on the doorstep
Life can be so sweet
On the sunny side of the street."

I responded by joining in with his voice; we harmonized just like we used to when we were married.

He pulled me up from a soft chair and started to dance with me, singing "I've Got a Crush on You." How could I have resisted him? So when he suggested we play a game of *Name That Tune* with Mom, I felt up for it. Mom was motionless but thank goodness she smiled when she saw Andy and me together. Soon she joined our little game. I love Mom's singing voice, and as sick as she was, she still had the strength to hum along with us. I used Dr. Holman's "Fantastic Fantasy" to help her move out of the present and into her good feelings. I began to hum "Fly Me to the Moon."

Frank Sinatra was one of her favorites. In her sweet melodious voice she sang the words to us, first softly and then with more energy. Andy started to sing on one side of the bed and I on the other... a trio of song birds.

"Fly me to the moon
And let me play among the stars
Let me see what spring is like
On Jupiter and Mars.
Fill my life with song
And let me sing forever more
You are all I hope for
All I worship and adore
In other words please be true
Andy lifted Mom up. I wrapped my arms around her.
In other words I love you"

Session #13 Journal #5
Forgiveness

Tonight it was just Mom and me. No Sara, no Andy, barely even nurses. It was late and I probably shouldn't have even been there. But it was so sort of seductive, the soft yellow light, the quiet, the deep halls with third shift nurses gliding by like the nuns at St. Martin's. Even they must have sensed something. They seemed to avoid Room 404 where my Mom and I sat holding hands; she with eyes shut, me with eyes wide, paying the closest attention I've ever paid to anything or anyone.

It was my eyes she must have felt, eyes that had grown wise and forgiving, loving and longing to understand her, understand me, and understand us. The depths, the fathoms that separate mothers and daughters, the depth and breadth and beyond that binds us. . .

She opened her eyes slowly as if out of some passionate embrace elsewhere, lids fluttering. She looked at me squarely once she focused.

"My dearest daughter, my only red-headed daughter," she whispered with a hint of amusement. She'd always said that, written it on cards, used it as a cover when I'd asked her who her favorite was. "You don't have any other daughters," I'd wail, "let alone red-headed ones!" And she'd smile, so tactful, so politically correct way before "politically correct" was even a blip on the social consciousness of the masses.

There was such a warmth in those pale eyes, those visitors from heaven. I said nothing. I waited. She gathered strength from resources she didn't have, to speak again. "Molly, dear, you are a wonderful mother to Sara. I wish I could have been that kind of mother to you. I'm sorry for hurting you. I loved you and I will always love you, but I never knew how to do it. I never knew how . . ."

Her voice trailed off, tired, sad. I took her hand as her eyes closed, and the tiniest tear ever escaped her left eye. As I watched it travel down her softest cheek, I was compelled to kiss it, catch it, taste it, hold it in my mouth like Holy Communion.

In her last moment, she was asking for my forgiveness, and with all the love in my heart I gave it to her.

Session #13 Journal #6
The Day Mom Dies

At 5:30 AM I called Andy and asked him to bring Sara to the hospital. As I waited, I felt my mom's strong, invisible threads, like those of the weaver spider, hold me captive.

For years and years I struggled to disconnect. Now I wish I hadn't been so critical. I hated her drinking so much; I never tried to understand where it came from. My feelings interfered with my being able to see the good things about her.

When Andy and Sara arrived at the hospital, I ran to him like a small child. I whispered to him that Mom was dead. When Sara saw my tears she knew. I cried instead of talking and Sara burst into tears just seeing my tears. Andy seemed stunned. We all clung to each other for quite a while.

Sara asked, "What will I do without my Grandma?"

Session #13 Journal #7
Molly & Andy Talk to Sara

It seemed there was just one thing we all wanted to do; snuggle on the sofa with Sara's comforter spread over us. Being together was all we could think about doing at the moment. Sara asked, again, in a very small voice, "What am I going to do without my Grandma? Andy just looked toward me.

Finally words came to me. "This is a very emotional time, a terrible time for all of us. We're going to help each other get through it."

Sara looked up with her red swollen face and asked, "How could she leave me? Do you think Grandma was drinking and that's the reason she died?"

I searched inside for the right answer for Sara… one that would give her solace. "Yes, you're right. I know the truth hurts.

Sara was crying and crying, "Grandma won't be able to take me to Paris when I turn sixteen."

Stroking Sara's hair and holding her close, I said, "I know, I know."

I looked over at Andy. He had a puzzled expression telling me he didn't understand what I was doing. I told him she had to get the anger out before she can go to sleep. Crying is helping her with the anger.

Sara put her head in my lap, her slow, sad tears drying as she closed her eyes. Finally, she sighed and I could feel her begin to relax. "Thank you Mom. I'm glad you're here Dad." Andy and I embraced with sympathetic eyes and hearts as we heard Sara's every breath. Her arms loosened around me and she started to feel heavy… within minutes she actually fell asleep.

Session #13 Journal #8
Molly Comforts Andy

After I comforted Sara, a terrible tiredness came over me. It was as if I had moved into an energyless realm. As I floated around the house aimlessly, I noticed Andy in the guest room, lying on the bed, a pillow over his face. He looked like a little lost boy. It broke my already broken heart to hear him repeat, "She was really the only mother I ever had." Andy seemed inconsolable. I had neither the tools nor the energy at that moment to help him.

After checking on Sara, who had not moved from the place in the bed where I left her, I made myself some hot milk. Even washing my face and brushing my teeth felt good – mindless ritual requiring no thought, no feeling, just doing. I'd choose to be a robot over human right now. But then I remember: my mother is dead. I feel so full of rage. Dr. Holman told me over and over the benefits of beating pillows on a mattress with fists or a rolled up towel to get the anger out. I've always been too embarrassed to do it and afraid of being out of control, but not tonight. Tonight I don't give a damn! I piled up pillows and beat the living hell out of them. I couldn't stop crying and beating. How angry I am that she's gone! It's too soon. I could feel my energy coming back. I felt like I'd released all my angry feelings. What is more upsetting than unexpressed anger?

The memory came back to me of what I had told Sara earlier. I began to remember some of the good times I had with Mother and Andy.

My mom used to be interested in Andy's and my camping trips. She wanted to know if we went fishing, what did we cook, did we sing around the campfire and who all went with us. It dawned on me that I would like to ask Mom on a weekend camping trip. Yes. Mom was excited to go so Andy made reservations at Carrillo Beach campsite. Andy bought a tent large enough for our little family. It was great! She loved it so much she asked to go with us again. I gave Mom the love I had been holding back for so many years. She seemed to have let down her reserved guard. I experienced a light-hearted fun Mom who talked to us, confided in us and asked us many questions from a truly interested place. The curious thing is that none of us seemed to miss alcohol. I wish mom could have felt safe enough to let down her guard more often.

My thoughts went to what's happening with Andy now. I decided to check up on him. I found him asleep, so I got into bed with him and held him. I felt like I had earlier with Sara, like the mother, and now Andy was my sad, little child.

Session #13 Journal #9
Sara's Eulogy

The morning before the funeral, Andy and I were in the kitchen making coffee when Sara came in upset and feeling left out. She said, "My grandma died yesterday and you two are talking secretly. You're leaving me out." She ran to her room and I followed after her.

"I know you are upset and I hear you! You want to be included in the funeral arrangements. What would you like to happen, Sara?"

She said, "I want to speak at my grandma's funeral. Mom, would you help me? I want to tell everyone how special my Nana was."

The next day, I was so moved by Sara's ability to go to the heart of each memory in her eulogy. Sara handled herself so maturely. Everyone cried.

I am -- I was -- my grandma's only grandchild. I knew how special I was to her because when I spent the weekend with her she would wake me up and we'd go to IHOP for health nut pancakes and crispy bacon. Then she'd take me to the bike path where we rode for miles. She liked to treat me to root beer floats before we came back. All these things she did for me made me feel so loved and that I counted more than anyone else.

In the early mornings I'd climb into her four-poster bed with the Italian lace curtains and mounds of icy blue satin down pillows and she read the children's classics. It took us six months to finish the *Tale of Two Cities*. She taught me to knit. She made a pale blue angora muffler that I treasure.

I'm so glad we finished the *Old Man and the Sea* because I don't think I would have finished it alone. It's one of those things meant for two people to do.

Best of all, Gram would play the piano and she was teaching me to sing. Oh, we both loved singing (belting out) American folk songs.

It was on the piano bench that I learned that Grandma wanted to be a professional singer. She gave up that dream for Grandpa because he felt that it was "not fitting." It was our secret that we knew he was afraid he'd lose her to a talented musician. He didn't like to sing or dance, but she never gave up wishing to fill her life with music and dance.

My mom told me that I have my own perception of Grandma in me that will always be mine. I love and cherished Grandma and her words to me, "Sara, you have the power in you to create your own wonderful dreams and to live those dreams."

Grandma – thank you – for giving me your wisdom and your love. I have you in my heart."

Session #13
Sam at the Funeral at the Back of the Church

Today at the funeral service, when I saw Sam standing in the back of the church all alone, my heart went out to him.. I had so much compassion for him and how patient he's been. I felt such love for him and then was overcome by guilt. It was a snapshot of how Sara and I have pushed him away from us, yet he still shows up, with love and concern but at a respectful distance.

I looked at Sam until I caught his eye. I pointed to the viewing line. He understood my message and went to stand in line to walk by mother's open casket. I quietly stepped in behind him. I wanted Sam to see my beautiful Mom in her final resting. She looked like an angel and I couldn't believe she was dead.

I was trying so hard to hold back my tears. Sam took my hand and squeezed it. We sneaked out a side door. He gave me a loving hug. I told him I would call him and I walked back into the church.

Session #13
Session after Mother's Death

M: Well, Dr. Holman, it's over! And I miss my mom so much. (her voice catches in her throat) I see her everywhere. I feel her presence. She's dead but she isn't gone. I see her when I look in the mirror. I see her in Sara. When I look in Andy's moon eyes, they glisten with tears.

You know, my mom meant so much to Andy because he lost his mother when he was two years old. The only Mom he knew was a very young secretary his father married right away. At 15, Andy was bereft when his father died. He had to bear it alone. He left his cold stepmother and went off to San Francisco right after he graduated from high school.

Since my mother is yet another loss for Andy, my heart really goes out to him. I want to console and comfort him.

H: I can see you've opened your heart to Andy.

M: These last weeks we've spent together have changed the way I see Andy. I'm surprised by my warm, caring feelings. I can understand now why our divorce was so hard on him. You know, Dr. Holman, I never put it together before. I wonder whether my releasing so much old anger –

H: . . .and re-discovering the treasure . . .

M: . . . led to how I feel about him?

H: What do you think, Molly?

M: (pause) It could be. It very well could be.

H: There is a great opportunity for healing here, Molly. Many people are afraid of death because they think of it as the end of good feelings. There is another way of thinking about death.

M: What do you mean another way of thinking about it? My mother is *dead*! I want you to show your compassion, I need your sympathy.

H: Yes. How would you like me to respond? I've seen how hard you've worked with your mother to get past your anger, to heal your relationship and to forgive and love your mother. And then she died. I understand that the feelings are very complex here – your feelings of anger, disappointment, sense of injustice, outrage, and yearning for the love you had and lost. It's unfair.

M: That's so true! It's not fair. (She starts to sob, then she looks up.) I held onto my anger with my mother for so long. I feel so terrible for having wasted so much time and I'll never have another chance. (She bursts into tears again.)

"Give me my mother back! I want my mother back!" As I recognized what I really wanted, I got so angry I punched the pillows in my chair. I felt like kicking, screaming, demanding, begging. Then I heard Dr. Holman's voice asking…

H: How would it be if you got what you wanted?

M: I'm standing in my family kitchen with my mother. She's making cream puffs. She smiles, puts her arms around me and says, "I love you, my darling daughter."

(To Dr. Holman) I got my mother back!

H: How are you feeling now?

M: I feel like my heart is open and it feels like heaven!

Journal #1 Before Session #14
Andy's Kisses Defy Death

In my late dusk darkening kitchen, you grabbed me and leaned yourself against me, kisses beginning, growing, flowering fat-mouthed and fast-motioned. I wanted your kisses to suck my mother's death out of me, take my lost lips in the bargain, take them into your friendly mouth, take my whole mouth into yours and swallow as you would take the sweetest summer peach and suck past the peach fuzz, suck sweetness out from me to you, feed yourself until you groan in succulent pleasure, take my breath and breathe, without fuss, just breathe me in all the way down, down to the bottom of you where I want to be, the bottom of you, the most bottom of your heart where they will never find me – I will be down there, kissing you from below, blowing kisses up to you, blown into a new existence like soft hot glass, clear and clean and full, warm, full of our breathing kisses, our breathing into morning light leaning into it, kissing ourselves alive. You kissed the low-lying dying out of me.

Journal #2 Before Session #14
After the Funeral

After the funeral I walked into the foyer of the house I grew up in. I was overwhelmed with sadness. The house was filled with family and friends, yet I felt so alone. I wanted to yell out, "Mom, where are you? Are you home? I need you!" I wanted to hear her voice respond to me in her sweet way. Oh, God, I miss her terribly. How am I going to get through the wake?

I watched Andy notice me standing alone in the hall, looking so sad. He brought over a hot cup of coffee and lead me to Mom's favorite wingchair. I sat there feeling deaf and dumb until someone put on an "oldie but goodie" and Andy gently pulled me up to dance. As he held me close, his long lashes brushing my cheek, I resisted my wish to melt into his arms.

Someone had found Mom's stack of old records and switched to one of her songs from the 40's. My mom and dad were great dancers in their day. I could picture them dancing in our living room to "It's Been a Long, Long Time."

Andy walked me over to the wingchair, saying he'd bring us something cool to drink. A sexy girl I recognized from high school tapped Andy on the shoulder as he was walking away. I heard her say, "Hi Andy, it's been a long time."

I couldn't hear Andy's reply, but I watched as she put her arms around him and whispered in his ear as they hugged one another. In that moment, I felt a flash of jealousy.

For the rest of the evening, I gave Andy the cold shoulder. Sara wouldn't leave my side, but kept signaling Andy to join us. I don't blame him for keeping his distance. I was so angry I didn't care if anybody wondered what "was up" between us. The embers of jealousy do not burn out easily.

Since I had worked on my jealous feelings in therapy, I thought I would never be caught by the green-eyed monster again.

Session #14
Andy and Molly with Holman 1st Session
Joint Therapy Session

H: What brings the two of you here?

M: Well, I don't know. What happened was that we started fighting at my mother's wake. I know enough now to know that what I say we're fighting about is not really what we're fighting about.

A: And I'd like to find out how Molly and I can avoid our old pitfalls.

M: What I've learned is that I fight because I'm angry. And I'm angry that things are not going my way. I want us to get along, but Andy, you spoil things. If only you understood how you do that, we wouldn't have fights.

A: Oh, it's all my fault.

M: I'm sorry! I didn't mean to blame you. The trouble is, I still can't resist getting drawn into it with you.

A: Yeah, I walked into the house to cook breakfast for you and Sara and wham! I ran into an iceberg. The next minute we were blaming each other and yelling. Sara started crying and begging us to stop.

M: Andy and I have been getting along very well these last few weeks. We dance, and talk heart to heart, we kind of rediscovered each other.

A: That's right! It makes me remember how wonderful Molly was when we were first dating. I realized I still had feelings like that for her, but then we had this fight. So, Dr. Holman, how do we stop?

H: In order for the relationship to grow and prosper it's necessary to let the anger emerge. But, the important thing is, you each have to find a way to do this without attacking the other. That takes learning some new skills. Are you open? In my system, we make the assumption that underneath the anger there are blocked good feelings. So the paradox is that each fight you have is an opportunity to express and get rid of the stored-up anger. Once that is done safely, you go on a treasure hunt to release the imprisoned good feelings. Molly, what is it that made you mad?

M: (to Andy) When I saw you carrying on with that girl . . .

A: Hey, I was just . . .

H: Can you hold on a minute, Andy? Would you allow me to talk to Molly first?

A: Okay.

H: Molly, what was it about Andy and the girl that made you mad?

M: That he didn't care about me or my feelings.

H: Since you didn't like what you felt was going on, how would you prefer it to be?

M: For Andy to come back with our drinks and to sit with me and talk to our friends and family. After all, it was my Mother's wake.

A: Oh, c'mon, Molly. I didn't know...

H: Excuse me again Andy. Molly, please imagine how it would be if you had gotten your wish.

M: Well, then I would have felt reassured that you care about my feelings.

H: If you think about it, what could you have done to bring that about?

M: After the hug, I was almost crying. I could have walked over to Andy and whispered, "Andy, I need you. I need you."

H: How would that be for you?

M: It would be hard, but I could do it.

H: How does that feel to you now?

M: I feel better.

H: Now, Andy, what made you mad?

A: I don't like being falsely accused. She said, "How could you be so insensitive to me?" And here I had been taking care of her all these past weeks.

H: It's clear Andy that you don't like what was happening. How would you rather it would have happened?

A: It makes me mad when she treats me as if she knows what I'm thinking, feeling, and why I'm doing what I'm doing.

H: And you don't like that!

A: Of course, I don't! Like I said! Especially when it's not true. And she hangs on to her belief that she knows the truth about me better than I do myself.

H: How would you prefer it to be?

A: I want her to ask me, rather than tell me what's going on inside of me. If she wants something of me, just to ask me.

H: Yes. Are you able to pretend you got your wish?

A: Hmmm! Well, I'll give it a try.

H: What is it you really want?

A: Well . . . She knows how much her mother meant to me. I would like her to acknowledge my loss, too. That would feel good.

H: Are you feeling that in your body?

A: Let's see . . . I feel lighter.

H: Molly, what do you think about what Andy just said?

M: It feels better to know his wish underneath the anger.

H: Andy, what do you think about what Molly said earlier, about her good wishes?

A: Oh, I like that! I would much prefer to hear her good wishes than to be the target of her justified anger.

H: (To Andy and Molly) Now notice that you have handled your anger in two different ways. The first way, that I like to call the old fashioned way, was what you did during your fight. The second way, that I like to call the new fashioned way, was where you changed your story: from what you didn't like to what you would have liked.

A: After I found my wish, and then I imagined I got my wish, I felt better.

H: So what you've done today is an introduction to the new fashioned way of getting to your good feelings. You both seem to have an attitude of good intentions. It may be a way, Andy, for you to get out of your "sticky mess." How did you like working together today?

A: This gives me hope that we can stop fighting and instead enjoy each other. I can tell you this--I'd rather feel good than fight!

Journal #1 After Session #14
Healing Anger with Andy

It is one in the morning. I have been awake remembering when my mother gave birth to my little brother, Charlie, and brought him home from the hospital. I remember how intensely jealous I was over the loving attention she gave him. She never even looked at me when she came through the door. I felt invisible to her.

As I keep working on my anger and jealous feelings toward Andy, I remember the many times Andy turned his gaze from me after Sara was born. He blamed and accused me for spending so much time at work and not paying more attention to Sara. I remember that I felt so jealous of Andy and Sara that I turned even more to my work. I was promoted to editor and then to senior editor. At least I felt proud to be making so much money and to be so successful at my craft. But it wasn't enough! I was on the wrong track. Finally Andy came to the decision that he was through with me *and* our marriage.

Until I went into therapy, I couldn't see that I was so focused on having Andy understand where I was coming from that I didn't recognize how much he wanted the same understanding from me. Andy started pulling away and I didn't realize that was a reaction to me. In my anger, I felt justified not giving sex to Andy. In fact, I didn't have any sexual feelings to give.

Journal #1 Before Session #15
Bathtub Fantasy

The thoughts that were running through my head before Andy came to my house were unexpected. "Is there any possibility that sex will be a part of the evening?" I allowed myself this fantasy about the movie to come:

I prepare to bathe in luxury by candlelight. I pay close attention to each part of my body, becoming my own man of the hour, looking at, touching ever-so- lightly, loving my breasts, my large nipples, pretending they are the breasts of Andy's dreams; soaping my inner thighs, pretending he is running his soft lips there, calling them the creamiest of white softness. I take time for each foot, each toe even, because I remember a former boyfriend kissing them, massaging them, making love to them, sucking on each one, speaking sonnets to them about their sweet pinkness, their softness.

I scrub every inch of skin, like the Japanese women (I've heard), bringing up the color, creating a tingling aliveness that is palpable. It invigorates and stimulates my imagination as I anticipate *his* touching me later, feeling the vigor and spirit beneath my skin, the pleasure that waits there, unearthly, close to the surface. I circle my body with an ocean sponge, soaps and bubbles and oils making smooth its path. This is of itself sensual and hints at what I want to happen later, preparing my psyche and my body for praise and adoration. Tapes of glory play in my head of how it is going to be, of how I am going to be, how I'm going to act, how he is going to respond in words, kisses, caresses, exploring out of a keen and natural curiosity, the satisfaction of which gives *him* pleasure.

The movie began when he came through the door and could see only my head above the bubbles. He walked confidently toward the bath tub, blew out all but two of the candles and stepped behind the claw foot tub, grabbing my curls as though they had been lost and he'd just found them. Those strangely lovely yet so masculine hands massaged my head. I couldn't stand it any longer; I motioned for him to get the towel. He started kissing me while he dried me off quickly. He continued to kiss me while he peeled out of his pants. He carried me into the bedroom and threw me down on the bed. It was the most important action he had ever taken. The care, the tenderness, the drive to talk with those hands, to tell me what I'd so wanted to hear, to give me everything he'd never thought to give me, to make up for all our doubts and fears of one another.

Andy did to me, with me, and for me what I had not been able to do for myself. He seemed to feel about me, about my body and about my beauty as he had never allowed himself to feel before. I received his gift: unconditional love and acceptance.

Session #15
I Love Two Men

M: I'm so glad to be here today. I've had more of those sleepless nights. Dr. Holman, I know it's a signal telling me something important is coming up from my reservoir, but I don't yet know what it is. What *I do know* is that I had an experience with Andy that shook my world.

H: Yes?

M: I think I'm in love with Andy. I can't believe it! How can I be in love with two men?

H: Would you like to fill me in a little?

M: I looked at Andy in a new way, as if I'd never seen him before. He looked so sexy! It sent me into orbit. I felt swept away! I felt so exhilarated.

What does it mean when I have those feelings with Sam, too? What's the matter with me? I feel like a flake. One day I'm in love with Sam, the next day I'm in love with Andy. Now I'm really in a bind. I feel so anxious I can hardly breathe.

Where did these feelings for Andy come from? Have I been keeping these good feelings down? Were they present during our marriage or are these feelings something new?

H: These are good questions to be asking. And how about another one like, "Have I become a more loving person?"

M: Well, I hope that's true! But then, why do I feel so anxious? I was so certain that Sam was the love of my life. What do I do with these feelings for Andy?

I feel warm just talking about him. My neck is hot, my ears are hot, and I feel heat between my legs. But the critics are breathing down my neck.

H: To cool you off? (Dr. Holman smiles)

M: (Laughing) No! They're putting me on the hot seat!

H: Well, perhaps you'd like to talk to these critics.

M: Oh no! I feel embarrassed enough. I can't stand to hear what they have to say. It's like listening to my pa...oh, I see. Well, the critics have been saying, "Have you no loyalty, Molly? How can you love two men? You know you've already made a commitment to Sam. You're just playing with Andy's feelings! You know you can't have everything you want in this life. Aren't you old enough to know you can't have your cake and eat it too? Your attitude and behavior are unacceptable to me!

H: Does that voice sound like one of your parents in particular?

M: (To Dr. Holman) Wow! It seems like my father's voice. It feels like he owns me.

H: What else do you notice?

M: No wonder I was afraid to speak up. No wonder I used to go along with everything he said.

H: How do you see yourself now?

M: As I stand back and listen to him, I believe he's more interested in having me do things his way than in what I think, what I feel or what I want. This is an aspect of my father that I never recognized. Or if I did, I pretended not to notice. I see how much I wanted to hold onto the image of my *idealized* father. And now, because of our work together, I'm not afraid to speak up to him. I recognize that I'm a separate person with separate feelings.

H: And now, knowing that, what would you like to say to your father?

M: Let's see... Daddy, I hear you're unhappy with the way things are going.

(Molly speaking as her father)

F: (in a louder voice) Molly, you simply cannot make love with two men! It's not normal. It's indecent!

M: (To Dr. Holman) Whew! I'm starting to perspire. Where do I go from here?

H: As you know, behind his anger, your father has a blocked wish. How can you find out what it is?

M: I remember now – the treasure hunt!

(To father) I hear you're very upset by what's happening.

F: Of course I'm upset! *No* daughter of mine would behave like you are behaving. Where is your loyalty? Why are you so fickle and flighty? Where is your sense of decency?

M: I can see this means a lot to you – you don't like the way things are. How would you like your daughter to be?

F: She would be loyal. She would be able to make up her mind and remain committed to her decisions. She would have character and dignity. She would be caring about other people's feelings. And above all, she would be respectful of her parents and their wishes.

M: I understand, Dad. And what would it be like if your wish came true?

F: Well, then I wouldn't have to worry about you.

M: And how would that be for you?

F: That would be a big relief. Then I'd know you have good values, that you know how to tell right from wrong, and we would have done our jobs as good parents. I wouldn't have to worry anymore.

M: And how would it be for you if you got your wish and you wouldn't have to watch over me or worry about me anymore?

F: (Taking a breath)   What a relief that would be!

M: And how does that feel to you?

F: I feel good. (He stretches out.)

M: Feeling that way, Daddy, what would you like to do?

F: What would I like to do?   To tell you the truth, Molly, I'd like to give you a big hug and whirl you around like I used to do.

M: (Giggles)   Yes, that's what you used to do when you came home from work, and I loved it.

(To Dr. Holman) That's my supportive Daddy.

H: What do you guess your *supportive Daddy* would say about you loving two men?

M: He would say, "I've come to realize that you, Molly, are able to make the best decisions about yourself -- better than anyone else."

H: Through the process of the Two-Chair Dialogue, you've become better acquainted with your image of your idealized father. In fact, you discovered two father images: the critical, judgmental teller, and the non-judgmental, supportive Daddy. You can let your idealized father-image fall away and deal now with the two different aspects separately: the "good father" and the "critical father." Can you tell me how you feel now?

M: I feel good all over . . . like smiling . . . and my anxiety has disappeared; I feel much more relaxed than when I came in. I have a better understanding of how I idealized my father. On the surface, I had so much adoration and love for him, but now I know I was also afraid of him. I had no idea how deep my worries of displeasing him were.

I realize I've been living as if he were still alive, and still demanding that I live like his perfect daughter. I haven't been living as the grown-up, independent person I *thought* I was. In fact, I've been living as if I still have to answer to him, haven't I?

H: In place of having your father be critical of you, would you like to turn him into an ally?

M: You mean choose the supportive, loving father and stop trying to please the critical father? Yes, I need an ally, not a critic.

You know, it feels wonderful to realize that I have another ally – Andy.

H: How would you say that occurred?

M: I've changed my view of Andy. Instead of needing for him to act out the role of my critical father, I've needed for him to be supportive and loving while my mother was dying. I've discovered that's who he really is.

Now I get how frustrating that had to be for Andy, to be seen and treated like someone he's not, and how angry that made him. One day he just said, "No more," and that's when our marriage ended.

H: And what about Sam?

M: It seems I've related to Sam as my supportive, loving father all along. Working with you, I've had new experiences which have helped me respond differently with Sam than I did with Andy. I am able to listen when he gets angry and continue being loving.

H: It seems your new self is doing the same thing with Andy this time around. Could that be why your good feelings have expanded to sexy feelings?

M: Ahhhhhh . . . But now, how do I explore my feelings for these two men without hurting them? That's my new dilemma.

Journal #1 after Session #15
Dilemma of Being in Love with 2 Men

Heaven help me! I am in love with two men! Sam and Andy & Andy and Sam. Now I can remember how wonderful I felt when Andy and I fell in love. When Sara was born we thought our love was complete. Was it all our reservoir anger that bent our relationship out of shape? I can now see that it was also our stupid old-fashioned beliefs that created our drama.

People talk about "coming to your senses," as if that were easy. Is there such a thing? Is it fair to keep Sara, Andy and Sam waiting for me to figure out what *I* want? What *do* I want?

During our marriage Andy would not put up with my shenanigans, but Sam's willingness to continue loving me no matter the ups and downs has helped hold us together. I think I need to reconnect with Sam before I can decide anything.

I'll have a heart to heart with Andy declaring my dilemma. I'm afraid Sara will be furious with me for choosing to go on a trip with Sam right now when she wants Andy and me together so badly. She's going to need Andy to comfort her. It looks like I'm going to be the bad mother for a while.

And what do I want? I do want to continue the search for the self that my buried anger has covered up. That means staying here, not going to Montana. Yet, I love Sara so much and I do love Andy; I feel so tempted to unite our family and go to Montana. Andy has changed and so have I.

Is loving Sara reason to give up the man I feel is my soul mate on so many levels? If I gave Sam up would I ever get over the loss? Am I the key to *their* happiness? Would I stop my work with Dr. Holman with whom I am changing my life for the better and better?

Journal #2 after Session #15
Still I love Myself

Dr. Holman is sometimes so cute that I feel like pinching his cheeks. Today when we were discussing those critical voices I've been dealing with for years, he suggested a quick way to handle those "nudges." He said as soon as I become aware of the critical or judgmental or "teller voice," I can say, "Molly, even though I love two men, still I love myself," putting my hand over my heart and repeating it three times.

He told me I could fill in anything in that sentence, like, "Even though I'm not perfect, still I love myself."

I'm thinking about how much energy I've spent putting myself down all these years, concentrating on my flaws. Can I give it up?

How about this one? "Even though I have these secret thoughts about you, Dr. Holman, still I love myself."

This is great! I can have fun with this.

Journal #1 Before Session #16
Sara's Blow Up II

This morning I had a shocking experience. I want to get down every word I can remember, so later I can think about it without being distracted by the emotions it stirred up in me.

Sara came out of her room and let her held-down feelings fly. She yelled, "You hypocrite! You haven't said one word to me about staying here or going back to live in Montana with Dad! I can tell you guys are carrying on. All those love looks between you! And your silly jokes, the way you both laugh 'til the tears run down your cheeks."

Her angry accusations really hurt.

"I hate your secrecy! I want to know what's going on between you!"

I felt unsafe with Sara for the first time in my life. She sounded like a jealous lover, and when I asked her what she meant by "hypocrite", she glowered at me.

She shouted, "You, the writer, don't know what a hypocrite is? You're manipulating two men, and one is my father. Isn't that true?"

At that point I invited her to go to my room for a heart-to-heart.

I told her, "I can see you're hurting. I know how angry you are. I really understand you want us to go live in Montana with Dad."

She yelled, "I want my family back! I want my family together!"

I asked, "And that would make you happy?"

She answered, "That's the only thing I want."

I asked her, "And you are afraid it won't happen?"

I was shaking inside. I knew I had to hold onto myself. I kept my attention on her. Then I asked, "Is there anything else you're afraid of?"

Sara became quiet. Then, almost crying she said, "Mom, I really don't understand about Grandma. I know what Grandma said. But who or what decides when you die? How do I know that you won't die next, or Dad? What about me?" She yelled, "I could die too! I hate it! I'm scared! I want us all to be together."

I took her in my arms to comfort her, to reassure her. In a moment she pushed away a little, and with her face four inches from mine, looked directly into my eyes and whispered, "Mom, I know you love me."

I whispered back, "Yes, darling, I do love you!"

She whispered, "If they decide that it's my time to die, will you stop them?" She waited, gazing steadily into my eyes, "Will you, Mom?"

So many thoughts and emotions came at me. Here was my only beloved child pleading with me to save her from Death. I wished with all my being that I could save her. No way was there room for me to say I'll try my damndest. No way could I fail. Yet I have no standing to command Death to spare her. I can't even do that for myself.

I knew that I needed to reassure Sara, even though I too am dealing with the death and loss of my mother. I told her, "I hear that you're worried about losing your Dad and me, and that something bad may happen to you. Let's remember that your grandmother did not take care of herself. Her over-drinking caused her fatal disease.

Now let's look at *our* family. *I'm* healthy and *you're* healthy and *your Daddy's* healthy, so you don't have to pretend those scary thoughts. We're here for you. Your Daddy's here for you. I'm here for you. We're going to take good care of you."

Now that I'm aware of the depth of Sara's fears, I can see why it's so important to her for all of us to be together in Montana. It makes me shudder to think that Sara has been worrying about death and she was afraid to talk to me.

Session #16
Molly and Andy with Dr. Holman

M:　　　Here we are again, Dr. Holman. It's a good thing you could see us today. We had a very upsetting experience with Sara this morning. We need your help.

H:　　　Alright, Molly. How can I help?

M:　　　(Starts to cry)　We're all mixed up. I'm so worried　about Sara -- I've never seen her so angry and distraught. She demanded that Andy and I declare our intentions. She desperately wants us to get　back together again.

M:　　　I'm feeling so many thoughts and feelings contradicting each other. I need to sort them out with your help, Dr. Holman. For instance, my mother didn't pay attention to my needs; I don't want to do the same to Sara. I want to pay attention to her strongly expressed feelings. Will I hurt Sara irreparably if I don't give in to her wishes about where she wants to live? Andy thinks we should go to Montana with him, but much as I love him, I'm not ready to go to Montana. It feels too soon after Mom's death. There's so much pain and regret to　work through, and too much grieving and growing to do to even think　about moving right now.

H:　　　Andy, where are you in this?

A:　　　Me? I don't understand you, Molly. You love me and I love you. We both love Sara. You say you want to grow.　Molly, for Pete's sake, who's stopping you from growing inside　of　our relationship? You and I are both older and wiser and more loving. Why can't you see, Molly, we all deserve this chance . . . unless it's about that other guy... what's his name?

M:　　　(Silence)　This is hard for me to say. I want to be honest and I don't want to hurt you. The truth is, before you came down here I made a commitment to Sam to be his girl.　Now you and I　have discovered a new love for each other, and I'm so very attracted to you. Don't you see, I'm in a terrible quandary!

A: So is this a competition? Sam or me?

H: Andy, from what you're saying, it sounds like you're feeling hurt and angry.

A: Wait a minute, Molly. This is crazy -- you already agreed to move to Montana.

M: What are you talking about? I never agreed to that! Where did you get that idea?

H: Hold on, hold on. (Pause) Andy, when you were thinking about coming here today, what were you hoping would happen?

A: I was hoping you could help us reunite our family, but now I hear she's involved with this other guy, I don't know where I stand. I feel betrayed. Molly, why didn't you tell me before?

M: I was afraid to tell you before. I was afraid I'd lose you.

A: Well, you just might!

M: (Crying) This is what I was afraid would happen! That's why I didn't tell you.

A: Well, what do you expect? I let my guard down with you. I felt we were really in sync -- at those moments we were the only two people in the world. Now I know that all the while you were thinking about Sam, too. Damn it, Molly! This is too much!

M: I hate it when you tell me what I've been thinking, especially when it's not true. If you want to know the truth, I was thinking only of you when I was with you. But I know you're not going to believe me.

H: If I may, I would like to tell you what I see is happening right now. You are each feeling angry, justifiably angry. Oddly enough, you are each accusing the other about the same behavior that *you* yourself are doing.

M & A: What???

H: You are each angry that your partner is accusing you of something that you believe isn't so. Furthermore, you each believe you're right and the other person is wrong. So you each feel misunderstood and unjustly accused and justly angry.

M: Wait a minute, Dr. Holman. I don't remember saying anything about Andy that wasn't so.

A: Oh, no? You just told me I wouldn't believe you, didn't you?

M: I did? Yes, I guess I was mind-reading you.

A: Sure! I'm glad you admit that! You're right, Dr. Holman. I get it. I was doing it, too. When I told Molly she was thinking about Sam while she was with me, I sounded like I knew her thoughts. Was I mind-reading her like she was doing to me? I'm not so sure! After all, when you're in love with a person for years, you get to know them, maybe even better than they do themselves. You get to know what they think and feel.

M: Ho! Ho! Ho! If only that were true! Then I wouldn't have felt so misunderstood and not listened to. You were always telling me what I felt, and acting as if you really knew, but you didn't. As a matter of fact, there were times I counted on you to know how I felt, only to find out you were way off track. What a disappointment.

A: Oh! What's the use? I've been falling in love with you, and I think you've been falling in love with me, and now there's this other character, Sam! You've brought up Montana and work and Sara, but you just don't want to leave Sam! That has to be it.

M: Oh, stop it Andy! You don't have any idea what I want and what I don't want!

A: How could I know what you want? You've been keeping secrets from me.

M: Yes, because I'm afraid of your explosions! I'm afraid to tell you what's going on.

A: So where does that leave me? Boy, do I feel like a fool. Every day I've fallen more and more in love with you. All I could think about was the three of us being together.

M: Until now, I was thinking that too!

A: You were? What about Sam? (He turns to Dr. Holman) I've had it! That's the Molly I used to know (pointing to Molly). I never knew what she was going to say or do. (To Dr. Holman again) Nice to know you, sir.   I'm leaving.

H: Just a moment, Andy. Please sit down. Maybe we can consider that this is a good place to be. We know that you each have justification for being angry, so now we have an opportunity to understand what's underneath this anger. What seems to be breaking this relationship may not be as it appears.

M: (Puts her hand to her head)   Oh, my God! Why did I get into this again? I know some new ways to do anger. I really don't have to keep blaming you.

H: (Speaking to Andy)   A short time ago, you felt loving feelings for Molly, right?

A: Yes, I did!

H: Do you remember the feeling?

A: Floating on air. Really turned on. Lots of sexy day dreams. Optimistic.

H: What stopped those feelings? How did those wonderful feelings get replaced by anger?

A: Just now, when I found out Molly was keeping secrets from me. Important secrets, like she promised herself to another man.

H: What happened? What did you do when you found out?

A: I got mad. I figured if she is really as afraid of me as she says, and she's got this other guy, why would she want to move away with me?

H: Is that a question or a conclusion?

A: A conclusion, I guess.

H: That sounds like a bad conclusion for you. How does it feel?

A: Bad. Terrible. Angry.

H: Is it possible that you could come to some other conclusions that weren't so bad?

A: What do you mean?

H: Considering that you made your conclusions based on incomplete evidence, is it possible that if you were to get additional evidence... what I mean is... Molly's *actual* feelings, might you come to other conclusions? Conclusions that would not be so hurtful to you?

A: But I did take into account her feelings . . . or did I? I guess I have to say that I considered what I *thought* her feelings were. Dammit, Dr. Holman, aren't we splitting hairs?

Wait, don't answer! You're telling me, or I'm telling myself, that there's a difference between what I know, or think I know about what she feels, and what she actually feels. Am I right, Dr. Holman?

H: Would you like to test it out?

A: How?

H: Would you be willing to ask Molly how she *really* feels? And compare it with what you *surmised* she feels?

M: (Going over to Andy, kneeling, and taking his hand.)

A: (Taking a deep breath) Okay, Molly. Tell me, how do you really feel about me? And about us . . . I'm listening.

M: Oh, Andy, I didn't mean for it to go this way. I adore you, and I know you're crazy about me in spite of all my short-comings. I don't think I've told you often enough how much you mean to me and how much I appreciate all the many ways you've helped us. (Framing his face in her hands and kissing him.)

(Molly returning to her seat) Here with you, Dr. Holman, I'm learning more and more about what I know and don't know.

(To Andy) What Dr. Holman calls "The Great I Don't Know."

H: Andy, do you understand what she means by "The Great I Don't Know?"

A: I'm not sure. I think she's saying she doesn't know and it's okay for her not to know. And she thinks that's a good place from which to find out. Right?

M: Right! You got it, Andy. That's where I am right now. I'm hoping its okay with you.

A: That does put a different light on it. I always thought that to admit you don't know means you're inferior; you've failed. We are supposed to know our own minds, aren't we?

H: Actually, by being aware that you don't know opens the doors to finding out.

A: And when I know what she is thinking and feeling, when I really *don't* know, I close the door?

M: Yes, you get it. You are the greatest! I'm learning there are so many loving places in you. You generously gave so much to my mother, me and Sara this past month. I'm so grateful for the way you took over with Mother's funeral arrangements. The way you were so loving with my mother helped me see how I could show my mother love too. I opened up loving places I didn't know I had. I am truly grateful to you.

A: (Going over and pulling Molly up, Andy puts his arms around her.)

M: Honey, I didn't mean for us to get into a fight. I'm really sorry I got so upset. What I really wanted to do was to let you in on what was going on inside me – all the wonderful and all the mixed up feelings.

A: I get you, Molly. I'm glad I stayed to hear you out. (Hugging Molly tightly) I'm going to try staying in "The Great I Don't Know."

Journal #1 after Session #16
No More Blaming Me or Andy

When Sara got so upset with Andy and me, and cried that she didn't know what was going on with us or where I stood about moving to Montana, I realized that I had been leaving her out, the way I was left out with my mom and dad.

Mom's serious illness has jolted my whole being. It's been like a huge thunderclap breaking the sound barrier of my reality. Thank goodness I have been in therapy with Doctor Holman. It's helped me stay grounded, to say the least. In his sweet gentle way, Dr. Holman has helped me see that anger is not a bad word or feeling, but a normal reaction when things are not the way I want them to be. I'm learning not to deny or push down the feeling just because it's negative. Over and over he says, "Let's get the anger out here in the office," and I have. I think that's what has helped me see the great person Andy is and why I feel so much love for him.

This work has helped me feel secure enough to face how I contributed to the demise of our marriage. No more blaming him or me.

Journal #2 after Session #16
At the Restaurant

I knew I had to bite the bullet. I was driving into Beverly Hills to meet Sam for our first reunion since the funeral. I recognized the symptoms of anxiety – the tightness in my stomach, my heart beating faster, my wet hands clenching the steering wheel. I wanted to tell Sam about the therapy session, about Sara and Andy and going to Montana. I was afraid this would be the last straw. I was afraid I would lose Sam now, just when we were able to have time to enjoy each other.

I felt caught between hurting Andy and setting off Sam's anger. Uh oh! These were familiar feelings. Fear. No wonder, I was pretending that Sam would be angry with me.

Waiting in rush hour traffic, I became aware that *I'm* writing this story! So how would I like it to be? My hands relaxed on the steering wheel and I started to smile.

Okay, since I was writing this story, I wanted to keep them both. In this story, they both understood and cared about my feelings. What else did I want? I pictured Sam hugging me in the restaurant, saying, "Honey, you've been through so much. We can go away next weekend. Then I can have you all to myself."

I felt proud of myself. I was in charge of my stories! Relieved, I walked into the restaurant in my powder blue jacket that Sam loves. With a big smile, I went straight to kiss him. He held me tight as I told him I had missed him so much. He said, "Not half as much as I've missed you."

It was hard to let go of each other when the maitre d' came to seat us. Now that we were together, I couldn't imagine how I had gone so long without seeing him and looking into his handsome face.

I held Sam's hand and told him how much it meant to me that he had been so patient and supportive, waiting in the wings while my mother was dying. He squeezed my hand and gave me another kiss.

Sam told me that while I was busy with my mother, he was throwing himself into his work and it was going to pay off.

"I am now Creative Director for all the advertising for Toyota."

I was thrilled for him and told him I believed he had it in him.

He asked, "What have *you* been up to?"

"Well, during the time at the hospital, I spent a lot of time with Sara and Andy. I found out he wasn't such a bad guy. My mother had greater understanding of Andy. She had lost her son, and he lost his mother when he was two years old. Me, I didn't have compassion for him; when I became angry, I had a cold attitude. No wonder the marriage didn't work. I've been continuing to see Dr. Holman and I'm taking responsibility for my part in our divorce."

"That's wonderful, Molly. You've done a lot."

"Mother didn't drink around Andy or Sara. I was always angry with my mother because she drank around me all my life.

Sam told me, "I can understand it. I had all those years with my father drinking. You and I make quite a pair."

"So Molly . . . it's been a rough couple of months. Is there a way we can go away for a few days?"

"Oh Sam, I'd love that. Andy's been dying to have Sara alone and she adores him. He's going to be leaving soon. Let me talk to him and I'll call you so we can make plans."

At home, getting ready for bed, I got butterflies thinking about calling Andy. I took a deep breath and picked up the phone. The hard part was telling him that I was going away with Sam.

I wasn't prepared for Andy's response. He said, "Molly, Molly. I told Dr. Holman I never know what to expect from you. You are something else." Then he laughed. "You know what, Molly dear, I'm gonna have a ball with Sara. As for what's going to happen between you and me, I'm going to try out 'The Great I Don't Know.'"

Session #17
Gem Dream

M: I had the strangest dream, Dr. Holman. I'm walking through a cool pine forest. I noticed a clearing ahead of me. I held my breath as a tall robed figure emerged from the mist. As he came toward me, I saw, cradled in his hands, a black satin pillow. He held the pillow out to me.

Beautifully displayed before me were two of the most magnificent gems I had ever seen in my life, a diamond and an emerald. Gazing at each sparkling gem, I felt a deep sense of awe. The mysterious figure nodded his head and simply said, "Choose!"

I looked at the diamond. The lights were dancing around, almost like a magnetic force, pulling me into its depths. As I reached for the diamond, my attention was drawn to the brilliant green emerald that must have been forty carats.

When I thought of choosing the emerald, I looked back at the diamond. A part of me was wondering why this mysterious stranger was putting me through this tormenting exercise? If I choose something wonderful, must I sacrifice something also wonderful? I started to turn away, then I swung around and confidently cried out, "I choose both!"

H: What happened?

M: I woke up.

H: How did you feel?

M: Elated. Victorious! A little anxious.

H: What comes to mind about the dream?

M: When the monk-like figure appeared, he seemed to have some kind of authority. When he invited me to choose one of the beautiful gems, I discovered there was no way I could choose.

H: What was it the figure said to do, again?

M: I remember very clearly. He showed me the gems and said, "Choose!"

H: "Choose?"

M: Oh, Dr. Holman… I thought he meant choose only one. I didn't want to. I couldn't! But he really didn't say that, did he? He could have meant to choose one or *both*. (She takes a deep breath.) Interesting how I interpreted him to mean I could have only one. Wait! How many times in my life have each of my parents told me, "Molly, you can't have everything." I'm hearing my Irish grandfather's voice as I'm reaching for another chocolate. He puts his big hand over my little one and asks, "Molly, ma darlin', don't ya think one is enough?"

Maybe I created the two exquisite jewels to represent a way out of my dilemma; I had to overcome the critical voices of my childhood in order to believe in myself. The dream is telling me I'm able to make the choice of what *I* want.

H: And what do you want?

M: I don't want to give up either one.

H: So you chose both.

M: Yes! In the past, I had to believe the authorities. Now I'm going to make a conscious vow to be watchful for those authority figures in myself. They sure cut down on my fun.

H: That sounds very promising. Good. Off the top of your head, what do you think your life would be like without the authorities and their rules?

M: Then I could trust myself to take charge of my own pleasure.

H: In your dream you came to a fork in the road. One path was to please the authority by doing as you were told. The other path was to please your own inner desire.

M: (Laughs.) Yes! I chose my desire. I chose both!

Here I am, strongly drawn to two men, wishing like crazy that I could have them both, thinking if I don't get my wish, my life will fall apart. All along, in my Inner World, I have had them both. I don't want to lose them in my Outer World. I need to express to both men what I want and what I don't want.

H: And then go from there.

M: What is Andy going to feel about Sam in my life, and what is Sam going to feel about Andy in my life? Like Andy said last time, as for what's going to happen between us, I'm going to try out "The Great I Don't Know."

Journal #1 after Session #17
How Clever the Unconscious Is

I'm amazed at how clever my unconscious is. It seemed so clear when I processed the jewel dream. I forgot how deeper layers continue to reveal themselves. There is more to this dream than the conflict of whether to choose Andy and change everything about my life, or choose Sam, stay in L.A. and reap the rewards of changing my inner life. I want to see myself grow into a more loving person.

I think my critics are having a hey-day with me. They are telling me that I should marry Andy and put my family back together. They say, "If you were a good mother, you would do what Sara wants. Why can't you get your priorities straight? Andy is a great guy and still loves you. Most women would not be so selfish." In a way I think "they" are right.

I'm noticing my mood is changing. So I won't ever have the love of my life . . . besides, good feelings can't last forever. Can't I see there is no other good way?

Oh-h-h, look what I'm doing. Holman would say that I'm going into agreement with my critics. No wonder I'm beginning to feel like going to bed. When I think of telling Sam goodbye, I want to pull the covers over my head and have a good cry. If I think of saying goodbye to Andy, I think of Sara and how my decision will affect her. I want to remember my vow not to be like my mother who never considered me or my feelings.

The "Jewel Dream" as I've started calling it was a perfect dream. When I transposed it onto the big screen, where it all felt real to me, it helped me see that I unconsciously created the authority figure. Then I resisted his command. It's no wonder I resisted. I could easily see that by doing what everyone had always told me, I became the victim, resentful and fearful.

At the end of the dream I felt powerful because I didn't give up either wish. I can see now how keeping both men means that I do not have to give up either. Whatever happens, I have the love for both men inside of me and it feels wonderful.

Journal #2 after Session #17
Loving Feelings

I love Andy so much. Even if he gets mad at me for not going to Montana, I still can have my loving feelings. They are mine! This is hard to write clearly. I'm going to keep at it anyway.

I didn't used to think this way about love.

I used to think Sam was the one who gave me my loving feelings. The way he made love to me, the way he was affectionate, the kindness in his voice, made me feel that he created the loving feelings I had for him.

Now with Andy – he, too, has been very caring, responsive to me in my time of need. I thought *he* turned me on, that his high sexual energy *made* me feel sexy and loving.

Now I understood neither Sam nor Andy make me love them. The love I feel for both of them is *in me*. It dwells in me. It wells up in me and flows out to them. I can love them whether or not I am with them, whether or not they are, at the moment, friendly or unfriendly.

I now have a different understanding about love and loving. What I do know is I love the way I feel when I feel loving.

Journal Instead of Session #18
Dialogue with my Dead Mother

I'm so glad all my dreams are not nightmares anymore. This one was the most intimate conversation I never had with my mother. It was so unbelievable! I better get it down on paper before I forget.

Molly: Mom, what do you think about masturbation?

Mother: What do you mean, what do I think about masturbation?

Molly: What I mean is what do you think about it. You know . . . whether it's right or wrong.

Mother: I don't think about it at all.

Molly: Well, I know, but I mean what do you think about its relative goodness or badness? I mean, do you think it's a bad thing? Do you think it's evil or wrong?

Mother: I don't know, Molly.   Why do you always talk about such strange topics?

Molly: Well, I've been thinking about talking to Sara, and I don't feel comfortable. I wanted to talk with you about it. I was just wondering how you might feel about something as controversial as masturbation in terms of morality. By the way, did you ever think about talking to me about it?

Mother: To be honest, I didn't. It's not the kind of thing we talked about.

Molly: Is it okay to talk about it now?

Mother: Up to now I've never talked about it with anyone – not even your father.

Molly: Have you ever done it or thought about doing it?

Mother: Oh, I suppose, when I was a silly high school girl, but we certainly didn't discuss it. And your grandmother would have stopped this discussion twenty five syllables ago!

Molly: Well, how about since you've been alone. I mean   since Dad died and all.   You mean to tell me that sex never crossed your mind?

Mother: Of course sex crossed my mind, but it wasn't something I dwelled on.

Molly: When it crossed your mind, did you think of sex with someone? Or did you think of doing it alone, satisfying yourself.

Mother: Oh no! It would be with a man … Mostly your father. No, to do it myself – I somehow believed only boys did that. We were taught not to touch ourselves down there.

Molly: But you were alone; you must have been lonely. Didn't you miss sex? You can't tell me you never feel turned on since Daddy died!

Mother: Molly, this is completely inappropriate. Your father and I hadn't had sex since shortly after your brother died.

Molly: Mom that was a long time ago. You mean to tell me you guys didn't have sex since then?

Mother: That's right.

Molly: Mom, c'mon. You've got to be kidding. I wonder, did you like sex when you were a girl?

Mother: Yes, I did. I can remember thinking that it was supposed to be bad but that *I* didn't think so. Besides it was fun doing things that would upset your grandfather had he known. He was such an old Presbyterian fuddy-duddy. He was so skeptical of your father and seeing his daughter so bothered and pre-occupied. It scared him, I think.

Molly: Was Dad a fuddy-duddy?

Mother: It didn't seem so at first. I guess, now that you mention it, he was a fuddy-duddy. I sure never thought so in the days before we were married.

Molly: Because?

Mother: Because we were so in love. We were so passionately in love.

Molly: I think I remember you telling me, a long time ago, that you were not a virgin when you and Daddy got married. Is that true or did I make it up?

Mother: You didn't make it up. Your father and I couldn't keep our hands off of each other. We would go out for cocktails and dinner with his musician friends and we would steal kisses and touches under the table. Everyone knew what was going on, but we pretended they didn't. As soon as the evening was over, we'd get into his car and start kissing. I led the way, I have to admit. Your father was such a prude, or at least he thought he had to be with me. He wanted to get married right away because his Catholic conscience bothered him so.

Molly: Were you reluctant?

Mother: Oh, heavens no! I couldn't eat or sleep for loving him. I could barely breathe until the next time we would see each other. It drove your grandparents crazy, especially Granddad.

Molly: Now that I know how much you enjoyed sex with Dad, it makes me wonder why I never saw you and Daddy hug and kiss, or well, you know . . .

Mother: Well, for one thing, that was how we were brought up. Somehow I got the idea that sex was for grown-ups, *married* grown-ups. Not for children. I believed that love making, in any form, even kissing, was only for us. For others to see it would diminish or tarnish it. I think I thought it would last if we kept it secret.

Molly: When I read about the Trobriand Islands, that really got me thinking. The Trobriand Islanders don't have any shame associated with sex. The parents are very happy with their mate – both as a friend, a lover and as head of their family. They are a happy, peaceful group. And they support their kids to experiment sexually as early as they wish. The kids have their own long-houses where they can play in private. The parents serve as models for good relationships so the kids feel free to discuss anything with them.

Mother: Sounds like you might have liked growing up as a Trobriand kid.

Molly: Well, I did think about it. I would have liked you to be like a Trobriand mother who could share your wisdom about what boys and girls can do.

Mother: What would you have liked me to say, Molly?

Molly: OK. Pretend you are a Trobriand mother. Let's see. Basically to tell me that sex was alright. More than just alright, it was natural, wonderful, healthy, given to me by God to enjoy – just as I enjoy laughing, jumping rope and pajama parties – and I can name a few more things – like chocolate fudge sundaes. When these good feelings would rise in me, I would know you know about them from your own experience, and that you love it and approve of it openly. And that I can always ask you about it.

Mother: That sounds good to me. I wish my mother could have said that to me.

Molly: If you were a Trobriander's mother, you would have modeled for me how beautiful and natural sex is. You would have supported my interests and activities. I would have felt free and curious and it would be easy to talk things over with you. It would feel so good to be open with you and know that you were open with me, that you didn't have to keep secrets from me . . . or from yourself.

Mother: That's a wonderful wish, my beautiful daughter. Thank you for sharing it with me.

Journal #1 Before Session #19
Before Cabo

I talked with Dr. Holman about the effervescence of my good feelings for Sam. I find it so easy to be with him. He's open, present, and it feels like he's non-judgmental, so I feel its okay to say whatever I feel or think. He may not agree, but instead of judging me, he leans toward me to hear how I view favorably something that he does not. It's amazing that we don't care about who is right or wrong. We care about finding out what each one thinks and feels. When he tells me about his inner thoughts and feelings, it's new and different. I feel included. I'm interested, right there.

When Sam asked me about taking a trip, I was ready. I said Cabo. He asked why. I said it has wonderful beaches, clear skies and I would feel good being only two hours away from home. He nodded and said that *his* fantasy was to take me to Hawaii. Warm water, private beaches, swaying palm trees.

We would hire a helicopter to take us to a private beach. Drop us off at 9 with a supply of provisions and pick us up at 6. We could play like we were castaways. Build ourselves a Tom Sawyer makeshift tent and play and make love all day.

I said, "Oh, our own private beach? I love the idea of being dropped off and have no civilized interference." I was able to tell Sam about my feeling of wanting to dry out my tears about Mother in the hot sand at Cabo. There was no tug-of-war. He just resonated to my deep, sad wish and agreed with me about going to Cabo. This communicating did not, of course, rule out either of our romantic, sexy anticipations.

Sam was tickled when I told him about my experience making the hotel reservations. When I asked for a king-sized bed, the concierge did not understand. He said, "Doble?"

I said, "No doble, camas! I wanted honeymoon grande camas."

"Oh, you want matrimonial, no?"

"Si, si – matrimonial. Si, Senor. We want the honeymoon suite."

Heaven knows what we'll end up getting. Now I'm feeling really excited *inside*. I can't wait to enjoy my romantic rendezvous with Sam.

Journal #2 Before Session #19
Arrival in Cabo

As we walked into our hotel room in Cabo, Sam exclaimed, "Wow!" It was a huge room with a deep blue ocean view showing through large arched windows. Sheer curtains veiled the matrimonial bed dressed in white. A table for two was set with pink hibiscus flowers.

The night tables held bowls of gardenias and candles that would light the night instead of lamps. White polar bear rugs covered the shiny bamboo hardwood floors.

No wonder he said, "Wow!"

The moment we were alone, Sam caressed my body, backed up to the bed with me in his arms, parted the netting, kissed me from head to toe and toe to head until I thought I was going to lose my mind. I begged him for more... more.

Finally, Sam announced, "Now it's time for a swim."

He grabbed my hand and we ran straight from the room to the cool water, playing and diving like dolphins.

Journal #3 Before Session #19
What We Like About Each Other

Sam and I took refuge from the sun by sitting in low beach chairs under a cabana. I turned my chair to face Sam, looking into his eyes.

M: I don't know another man that would have the patience to wait on the sidelines while my mom was dying. I asked you to wait for me and you did wait, not knowing how long the process would be. I'm so grateful for your kindness and patience.

S: Thank you, Molly. I appreciate your acknowledgement. It wasn't easy, especially when Andy was there with you everyday. I didn't even get to meet your mom. I was concerned that I lost you when Andy made all the funeral arrangements and gave the eulogy as if he were her son.

M: Oh, I know! When I saw you in the back of the church at her memorial, standing alone, my heart ached for you. You were supportive and understanding when I didn't invite you to the wake. I felt so pulled, wanting to be with you but leaving you out. What a drama I created for myself, and you don't even know the worst parts of the wake. Someday, I'll share what happened.

S: The best part of the story is that you're here with me now. My sweet Molly, you've been through so much. I brought you here to relax and have fun, and that's what we're going to keep doing!

Like children we challenged one another to a race to the ski boat platform. Upon our return to the shore, Sam grabbed me and gave me a smooch on the lips. I tripped over a rock and with peals of laughter we hopped over the sand. Sam wrapped me in a towel and bundled me up. We ordered cold drinks. Sam snatched the suntan oil from me and said...

S: This is my job.

Sam poured the suntan oil down my back and I squealed.

M: Where else are you going to pour the oil?

S: Close your eyes, Molly, I promise I will be discreet. Allow yourself to enjoy the soft buttery oil as I surprise your senses. I love to watch your face as you relax and purr at my strokes.

M: Your hands, the lotion and the hot sun feel so good.

S: One of the many things I love about you, darling, is the loving way you respond to me.

M: What else do you love about me?

S: Off the top of my head, I have noticed some changes that you've made. Since our "bottle incident" you don't accuse me and make me the bad guy.

M: What's different is I'm not giving you the power to make me happy or sad, like I used to. I think I'm learning my lesson now. I'm so ashamed of the way I flew out of your house and accused you of hiding the bottles. I behaved like a wild hysteric. I promise never to act like that again.

S: I do remember a time you had strict rules that were very important to you.

M: Yes?

S: So important that what was important to me seemed not to count with you.

M: Are you referring to when we first met?

S: Yup!

M: That is amazing. That is exactly how I felt about you. I'm so glad I hung in there.

S: I'll admit I felt and saw something uniquely different in you, Molly, and that something pulled me back into saying yes to calling you again. I wonder, would you have called me if you hadn't heard from me?

M: Yes, those soft sweet kisses felt like nectar from the gods. I would have eventually calmed down and given in to the thrill of your voice, those sweet kisses, your strong arms . . . I melted.

S: We do have combustible chemistry that will help us in rough times.

M: I feel secure in that knowledge too, Sam.

S: Let's get back to what I love about you, Molly. The more I look at the positive stuff in you the happier I feel. I really love that you did not react to my being jealous of Andy. You were so understanding and sympathetic. I think the fact that you continued to be loving helped me.

M: Oh Sam, you mean so much to me. This is really hard but there's something I need to tell you. I don't want secrets to come between us. I need to tell you that my relationship with Andy changed over the last couple of months. I can't justify it, it just happened. Sara and Andy want us to move to Montana and be a family again.

S: What are you telling me?

M: I told Andy how important you are to me and that I'm not willing to move to Montana. I want to spend time with you.

S: I'll be honest, I feel jealous. Before, I would have blown up. I know you've been spending a lot of time with Andy and I must admit, this has crossed my mind, and I hate it. When I felt jealous about Andy before, I believed my story that you didn't care about me, but I know you really do.

M   I don't want to lose your love. I feel worried telling you this.

S: It's hard to hear about your relationship with Andy, but   you are telling me about it even though it's difficult for both of us. Not everyone would do that. It puts our relationship on a new footing with an honesty I haven't experienced before, and that feels good.

I don't know where this is going, but I love you and you love me. Let's continue on and have the good time together that we both deserve!

Journal #4 Before Session #19
Spin the Bottle

M: Sam, are you awake?

S: I am now.

M: I want to tell you how much I'm loving the morning after. I'm loving the feeling of the cool ocean breeze caressing my body. (Sam wrapped me in his arms and kissed me passionately.) Ooooooooooooo, wait, I'm hungry. Shall we order room service? We haven't done that since the big earthquake. (I giggled.)

S: Did we have room service that night? I was passed out!

M: Did we have room service? Yes! I ordered a feast and when the poor waiter delivered the cart with our two dinners he stared at your nude body sprawled on the top of the bed, and me flushed from my hot bubble bath and starving.

S: That was when I was drinking and celebrating, and now I'm just celebrating. Come here my gorgeous, sexy woman.

M: (Giving Sam a kiss.) After last night, being open and being ourselves, I think we've discovered a new dimension of love.

S: It's true.

M: (Hanging up the phone after ordering a big Mexican breakfast) So Sam, now I want to hear some of your secrets. How old were you when you first knew about sex? When and where? Tell me everything!

S: I'll tell if you tell.

M: (giggling) I could be persuaded…

S: I was ten years old. It was a hot summer night and I wanted to sleep in a tent in the backyard. I invited my best friend, George, who was also ten and lived next door, to sleep with me. Laura, another neighbor, soon came over and crawled in with us. She sat between George's legs to make room for the three of us. She suggested we use the flashlight as a bottle and play spin the bottle. I didn't want to kiss her so she came over and sat in between my legs. When we turned the flashlight on George, he had taken out his penis. I said to Laura, "Let's not kiss, let's play 'touch this'." When she hesitated, I dared her. Just then my Dad pulled back the flap of the tent. Laura screamed and Dad yelled. He silently took the tent down as Laura and George went home. Nothing was said! Okay, it's your turn.

M: Well, mine isn't as exciting as yours. It was Saturday morning. I came into my parent's room to ask if I could watch cartoons. I gasped when I saw my dad on top of my mom. Her eyes were closed and she was moaning. So I yelled at Dad, "Stop hurting my mom!" Daddy replied, "I am not hurting her. I am loving her." After a few moments, Mom came out in her bathrobe and we went into the kitchen. She made me hot chocolate and told me that Dad was loving her because they were trying to make a baby. I told her emphatically, "I want to be your only baby!"

S: You've come a long way, baby!

M: Looking back, I just realized they were "covering up" their pleasure. Hmmm, I guess that's where I learned to cover up *my* pleasure.

Journal #5 Before Session #19
Love and Lust

Oh my, when love and lust come together....how do I do justice to sex so sweet? Sex jam-packed with love. The poet, Rainer Maria Rilke, advised his student poets to leave the writing about love (and its side kick, sex) to the elders. But I'm still young. Sam's young. And I'm compelled to write about our sex last night.

It started by my confessing to Sam a few more of my secrets. I told him about the night of the earthquake, about what I did while he was asleep, stories I must have been too ashamed to tell before. Holman has me convinced that honesty is a privilege, a gift. If I honor the truth of who I am, and with a trusting heart share it with Sam, then I am the lucky one. It is a privilege to be honest with Sam, truly intimate. In the telling I felt a surge of liberation. I was no longer ashamed of my complete abandon in the height of sex. I no longer made Sam my critic. Because my heart and mind are coming together, my "higher self" got so turned on.

As I talked, I could also see Sam getting aroused. Seeing him twitch and shift his body, trying his best to listen attentively and not give in to his erection made me shiver. My words were like kisses, his listening was like touch, and soon we were kissing and then we were touching with no need for words. I have never experienced myself or my heart feeling so connected to sex. Sam's touch, his alternating soft and rough touch, reached me like never before. I surrendered.

Journal #6 Before Session #19
Intimacy

Last evening in hotel on a hammock on the patio . . .

M: I've never seen shooting stars like this before. I experience the universe like never before because I feel so close to you, to your heart beat, to your heart. It allows me to open up.

(silence)

M: I wonder why you never married . . .

S: Because I've been waiting for *you*!

M: *(Kisses him)* No, really! Tell me!

S: Well, when I met you, I realized there had been something missing with other women.

M: What were you looking for?

S: A woman who didn't challenge everything I said – who accepted my thoughts and didn't need to make me wrong.

M: Uh oh, I'm afraid I've done that with you a lot.

S: Don't worry about it, sweetheart; you hardly do that anymore. Besides, if you do, I'll let you know.

M: Okay. Go on . . .

S: I don't like jealousy in a woman. I don't like a woman who becomes silent saying, "Nothing is the matter," and when I beg her to tell me, accuses me of something I don't know anything about. You aren't afraid to speak up in the moment. In the beginning there were a few things that were similar to other women.

M: Like what?

S: Like being critical and then righteous. But after you started talking with Holman, I noticed changes. At first you acted as if you knew what I was thinking and feeling and I didn't like it. Then you started asking questions as if you didn't know but you were interested in finding out.

M: It sounds so good to hear you say that.

S: Me too!

M: *You've* changed a lot through *my* therapy.

S: I also see now that my need to be right was a big factor in spoiling my relationships.

M: You know, Dr. Holman talks about three coping systems that we use in a relationship. One is fear and protection, one is manipulation and retaliation and the last one is love and growth.

S: Well, I go back and forth between all three!

M: Yeah, so do I but at least I'm aware of it now.

(pause)

S: Let's get married!!!

M: Are you serious?

S: Yes, I'm serious. I want you all to myself. No Andy.

M: I don't want to lose you either, sweetheart.

(pause)

M: How about we just continue loving each other.

S: I'll settle for that.

Session #19
After Cabo

A few days after we got back from Cabo, I had my regular appointment with Dr. Holman. He gave me a big hug when he saw me and said I looked healthy and vibrant. I told him what a wonderful time we had.

M: The last two nights since I've been back, I haven't slept. I don't know what's bothering me.

H: Did you have any dreams?

M: Yes, I did, right before we left Cabo. Now I remember. It was so strange -- I got a call from Ireland. It was from Sam's ex-wife. She said it was an emergency, but Sam wasn't in the hotel room. She told me their child had pneumonia and to complicate matters, their little girl had a hole in her heart which required surgery immediately. Because the dream was so upsetting, I didn't tell Sam about it when I woke up.

H: Why?

M: It felt so real. I'm afraid of sounding jealous of a wife and child that don't exist when he's been so patient with me, my daughter and my former husband. How could I be jealous? Anyway, I didn't want to spoil a great weekend.

H: Are you confusing Inner World with Outer World? We've talked about the effect of secrets on a relationship. Instead of being open, you chose to be closed as if the dream were real.

M: (Pause) Yes, I am. I was so angry and hurt and jealous that he kept such a big secret from me, and devastated that he was going to have to leave me.

H: You know that all these feelings came from the dream. They weren't real, so why the secret?

M: This is where I get into trouble, the difference between Inner World and Outer World.

H: Are you letting the Inner World fears affect your Outer World relationship?

M: Yes, I'm afraid of losing all these good feelings that Sam and I have shared in Cabo. Now I'm back in my real world, I want to protect the loving feelings.

H: Well, let's play it out. Do you want to close your eyes? After sharing the dream with Sam, what do you think he would say or do?

M as Sam: Oh, you silly girl. I would never have a secret life. I don't want to hide anything from you. I want to be open.

M: What a relief! I'm very happy to hear you say that. I was so afraid to tell you.

M as Sam: Poor Molly. You're getting confused. (He takes me in his arms and hugs me.) I'm the man who loves only you. I would never hurt you.

H: How are you feeling now that your secret is out?

M: Relieved. Supported. Loved and loving. I realize I miss out on good feelings when I choose to hide or keep secrets.

Journal Before Session #20
Taking Andy to the Airport

Last night my angel, Sara, needed me and I loved holding her again as she fell asleep. Then Andy came in and said, "Move over Molly, I want to talk to you.

"I feel small and lost. I hate to admit that I need you, your strength, your good sense. I used to be a pillar of strength."

I took him in my arms like I did Sara. I stroked his head. I brushed away his tears and held back my own. My heart hurts, and although the decision not to go to Montana seems right, I ask myself, "Am I making the right choice?" Life and love are so complicated. There he was, this big strong man needing me.

I held him in my arms until he fell asleep. I knew I had to get to my own bed before I could sleep. I extricated myself carefully from two needy children. *This* mother needed her rest.

Getting ready this morning to take Andy to the airport felt like a slow motion scene in a movie!

Sara cried, "I don't want you to go, Daddy. I want to go with you."

He had big crocodile tears in his eyes. He couldn't talk.

Sara took her favorite teddy bear out from under her coat and silently handed it to Andy. He bent down to hug and kiss her. He said, "My special darling, Sara. I love you."

I said, "Don't worry, Sara. We'll see Daddy sooner than you think."

At the airport, before Andy checked in, we looked for an empty bench. I hugged Andy and asked, "How can I thank you?"

Andy said, "I did what I could for all of us. I wish I didn't have to leave."

"Andy, I have something to tell you."

He held up his hand, "I know, I know."

"When I love somebody, I feel it's forever. I have the deepest feelings for you that go beyond this world. And I need to be free without limits.

Andy kissed Sara's tear-stained face all over. "Are you worried that you won't see me enough?"

"Yes."

"Oh honey." Andy bent down and held her.

I couldn't keep from crying. He gave me a passionate kiss, said, "So long kid," and with a wave he was gone. We missed him already. I couldn't imagine home without him.

Session #20
Loss After Andy Leaves in Holman's Office

M: I had a few of those sleepless nights, again. I'm definitely in love with two men. One is my Knight in Shining Armor, truly caring about my mother, Sara and me. He even seems open to my wish to be free. Then there's Sam, who's been patient and wonderful, standing on the sidelines, while I spent weeks with my former husband. Sam and Andy both want to claim exclusive connection to me. If I'm not thinking of marriage, can they appreciate me as I am?

Since Andy's gone back to Montana, I'm spending time with Sam again, but everything's different now that I have loving feelings for Andy, which I haven't wanted to think about. Do you think this is why I'm not sleeping?

H: Yes.

M: Well, I had no idea I was going to have sexual and romantic feelings for Andy! Like that afternoon I came home from work, when Andy looked so sexy, he aroused feelings in me I never expected to feel for him. Now I'm overwhelmed by all these sexual feelings for both men. I love the feelings, don't get me wrong. Is it the thought that something bad will happen to me that's keeping me up at night? Or is it the old feeling of loss that's keeping me awake?

H: Something bad...what are you thinking?

M: I could be punished for loving two men. Andy could get upset and never come back or Sam could become angry with me and leave me.

H: Have you given away your power?

M: Oh, I see. I've given them both the power to leave me.

H: How does it feel?

M: It feels real.

H: Inner World or Outer World?

M: Ahhhh! I'm making up a story in my Inner World. I need to take back my power and think about how I'd like it to be. I'll do it now. (Molly closes her eyes.) Andy is whispering in my ear, "I haven't gone away. I'm right here beside you ..."

(After a few moments)

H: How do you feel now?

(Embracing herself, Molly rocks back and forth.)

M: It's very comforting.

H: Notice how you have your arms wrapped around yourself, rocking... you can care for yourself in that way anytime you want to feel comforted.

M: Even though this feels good, the thought of telling Sam about my deeper feelings for Andy scares me to death.

(Pause)

H: In the past were you afraid to speak up to Sam?

M: Yes, I was, but not as afraid as I feel now.

H: How did your father express anger?

M: His anger was unpredictable. Most of the time he was happy- go-lucky like Sam. The times my father did show anger, he seemed out of control. That was very scary to me.

H: Can you remember an experience when you spoke up to your father and it didn't turn out well?

M: Well, let me see ...What comes to mind is the spring before I graduated from college. I innocently shared my plans for spring vacation with him. I told him that Peter, my boyfriend, and I were going to Hawaii with the gang. All of a sudden he flew into a rage and yelled "No! No! No!", while he moved toward me. The room turned upside down; I thought I was going to faint. He turned on his heel, slammed out the front door, and I didn't see him for two days. These incidents happened more often than I care to remember. I'm sure I've pushed these frightening memories deep down in my reservoir.

H: How are you feeling in your body right now?

M: My hands and feet are cold. I was getting very tense.

H: Would you like to take a few deep breaths?

(Molly taking a pause and breathing)

H: Do you feel calm enough to practice talking to Sam?

M: Talk to the real Sam? No – I'm not ready.

H: I'm sorry. I mean your Inner World image of Sam, in the chair.

M: That sounds better.

Session #21
The Victim Returns

M: You know, Dr. Holman, I realized something disturbing while I was in Cabo; sometimes I still feel justified in being angry with my mother. Because of her drinking and what she did to my childhood, I can return to feeling like a victim. P-o-o-r me.

H: When you notice yourself moving into the role of victim,   are you aware of why you're feeling angry, aware of your blocked wish?

M: I understand from our work where my anger came from,   that it's not from what my mother did or did not do; it's from not allowing my loving feelings for her when she disappointed me.

H: You've described how you responded when you wanted her and she was distant.

M: Yes, I'd pull away and take my good feelings with me. Now I see I had other choices. For example, when I'm distracted, Sara doesn't withdraw her good feelings. She will ask me to play cards   or bake cookies with her and then my focus shifts to her, and we both feel good. I never thought of doing that with my mother.

H: Now you're aware of the bigger picture that behind   the depression and withdrawn attitude is a happy loving person.

M: Yes. I wish I'd seen your big picture sooner. I've botched   a lot of things.

H: Molly, you've trusted yourself to handle everything that ever happened to you, one way or another.

M: Wait! What do you mean?

H: Does it make a difference to you if you say "I handled it badly," or if you say "I handled it."

M: Okay, let's see…if I say to myself, "I handled it badly," that's a judgment. A negative judgment. If I say,   "I   handled   it," it's incomplete. Something is missing.

H: The negative judgment is missing.

Journal #1 instead of Session #22
Going to Malibu

While finishing my monthly article and signing off on the photos, Sam called from downstairs with a surprise invitation for a weekend in Malibu. I became a whirlwind getting out of the office. On this gorgeous Friday afternoon, Sam dropped me off at home to quickly pack a bag while he made a run across town to pick up the key to his friend's beach house and to grab a few things for himself.

I smiled as I packed my favorite lingerie and a new bottle of almond massage oil. Being spontaneous isn't quite as easy for me as it is for Sam, but I was delighted when Sara's quick plan to spend the night next door worked out without a hitch.

An hour later, Sam threw back the top of his new convertible and tossed my bag in the trunk. We leaned against the car, kissing like long-lost-lovers. Finally, we started out for Malibu.

The mild winter Santa Ana winds seemed to move the open car as if it had sails for power. Feeling the sails billow and float, I floated, too. I released all thoughts until I was one with the wind. I realized I needed to keep breathing, slower and deeper. Releasing all the tensions, I watched my breath empty my thoughts and felt deep pleasure. I was amazed how well the breathing worked. I felt lighter and freer.

My trust in the work I had been doing with Dr. Holman seemed to make life richer, deeper and calmer. I felt more confident to turn difficult experiences around in ways I never knew were possible.

Not to say that I didn't feel guilty after Sara's temper tantrum, but I didn't let the guilt make my decision for me. I didn't choose to go back to Montana to become a family again just because of Sara's anger. Andy and I truly did have fun, laughing until we were sputtering, seeing our deep connection in one another's eyes. And then there was the incredible joy I shared with Sam. I was lucky to have two great guys who really cared about me. But what felt the best to me was that I could allow myself to care so deeply about them.

I felt as if I had been pulling a caboose full of questions up a mountain, inch by inch, feeling panicked that the heavy red caboose might roll down the mountain out of control. I looked over at Sam. His face looked relaxed and happy. I took Sam's hand in mine and placed it over my heart. I was thinking how much I enjoyed the silence. Sam seemed to understand. Lately we felt in tune. I wanted to make this time all about Sam and me. I realized I hadn't even heard him singing a love song to me in his deep, melodious voice.

"You mean everything to me," he sang. And I sang back to him. Back and forth we went until we reached Malibu. Just before the bridge, we stopped for a red light. He was signaling for a right turn. "I want to take a small detour," he told me. Sam turned in at Cross Creek Shopping Center. "I need to make one stop."

He was grinning as he pointed at me and said, "You wait here."

Moving with a quick step, Sam disappeared into Malibu Home and Bath. Later I discovered he had chosen two luxuriously thick white terry robes and some of my favorite aromatherapy candles. Returning to the car with his surprise purchases, we smooched like kids again.

In response to a honking driver impatient for our parking place, we dissolved into laughter after yelling in unison, "Hey, we're in love!"

Sam held up the key, teasing me as we raced to the front door of the Malibu beach cottage. He got there first, unlocking and throwing the door open in one movement. We both expressed astonishment at the unexpected splendor of the wall to wall sparkling royal blue ocean. It was some time before our attention turned to the house itself. River stone fireplace, comfy cushions on the hearth, the deck with bench swing and blue umbrella, fresh towels and beach sandals just waiting for us.

We went upstairs to the master suite to put on swimsuits, but suddenly changed our minds when we saw the huge white down bed. We fell onto it as one, in the spontaneous passion of freedom.

Alternating between hot love and damp naps, we arose, wishing for the coolness of beach air and a dip in the sea. It was late afternoon, when the sunlight changes from bright yellow to mellow orange, when the water takes on a silvery aquamarine hue.

We ran from the water back to the house, famished. Flinging open the huge stainless steel doors of the Subzero, we discovered an array of mouth-watering snacks.

Wet-suited, we fed each other fantastic morsels, devouring our happy feast while freezing in front of the open refrigerator doors.

A hot shower came next, rubbing each other to warmth with sea sponges and green algae shower gel. We shampooed each other's hair, making those funny sculptures with thick suds and heartily laughing at how ridiculous the *other* looked.

Unable to pass the bed without hearing its call to pleasure, we began a slower, timeless touching.

Journal #2 instead of Session #22
3AM in Malibu

I came awake at 3:00 A.M. My first thought was to snuggle with Sam and make love but he seemed so blissfully asleep, I decided to get out my laptop and write.

Last night, when we returned from our walk on the beach, he wrapped me in my new terry robe, made a hot fire, and then took my cold feet between his warm, muscular thighs. Ahhhhh, bliss. I felt so loved and cared about.

As Sam sleeps, I'm writing downstairs, the fire still glowing. The living room of the cottage is lit by soft lamplight illuminating the large sheepskin rug covering the floor, comfortable blue denim down couches, a large red wingchair by the fireplace and a long black-lacquered coffee table where we take our meals. I look like I'm in a Norman Rockwell print. What a wonderful realization that I've moved beyond my old fears. Tonight, Sam is the man of my dreams. He knows what I want and gladly gives it to me. I like the new Sam so much; he's made so many changes. It feels like we're more loving to each other. We no longer need alcohol to reach this state of pleasure, and I don't miss it. Hurrah!

Over these months I've realized how I used alcohol and food to avoid getting undressed. I was afraid to let Sam see me naked because I was sure he would judge me; but also, down deep, I was afraid he'd get turned on, and be interested only in my body, not in me. Then I was afraid I'd have to perform. I would be stuck in doing my old song and dance. I was afraid there was no way out for me. I would not live up to his expectations.

Where did my old fears go? What a wonderful realization – that I've moved beyond those old fears. For now I'm remembering that there's even another fear – that I was sinning with all those nuns watching. I was condemned to hell. It makes me shiver to know that I believed that story so thoroughly.

It's so wonderful to be able to share with Sam these deeper secrets that I have been uncovering. I feel so good loving him. I'd like this feeling to continue forever.

I'm still not feeling sleepy. Maybe I'll try Dr. Holman's suggestion for finding out what's going on inside of me by asking myself questions.

Questioner: You really want to know what's going on? You won't be mad at me if I tell you out loud what I see?

M: Hmmmmm. Honestly, I'm not sure. I'll have to find out. What's your emotional attitude toward me? Are you my loving helper, or are you a critic or judge tallying up my flaws that I've tried to keep hidden? I've had too many people come at me with "well-meaning advice" which I recognize now as a mixture of love and anger.

Q: I see I need to gain your trust. So trust yourself. Let's get started. What would happen if you tell Andy you're not going to marry him?

M: You mean now or never? I'm afraid he would be angry and storm out like he did when I told him about Sam. I'm afraid that Sara would never forgive me. I would mess up her life.

Q: What would happen if you tell Sam that you're not going to marry *him*?

M: How could I possibly tell my darling Sam who's waited for me so patiently? After all I've put him through?

Q: You did tell Sam you weren't ready to marry anyone, but when you were ready, he would be the one.

M: Oh I see. You're right. I didn't understand what I've done to myself. I put myself in a position with no way out. I can't tell Andy and I can't tell Sam. My old coping method would be to deny the truth and take a nap. But that's how I've arrived here. How could you do this to me? You've been watching all along. Now what should I do? Where have you been?

Q: You've been so content with your loving thoughts that you didn't put yourself in Andy's shoes and didn't put yourself in Sam's shoes.

M: You're right. But it felt so good to feel good. Now I feel sick. What am I going to do? I can't make a decision. I feel so terrible.

Q: Your life has become complicated.

M: I remember when Andy said to Dr. Holman, "What's the problem? She loves me and I love her and we love Sara." He would be a politician, we would live on the Ranch and Sara would have her own horse. We would live happily ever after. That was his fantasy.

Q: What was your fantasy?

M: Mine is to be free! Mine would be not to marry anybody. I would continue to write for the magazine and that opens up all kinds of possibilities for me. Sara and I will develop a unique relationship with understanding and love. My dear Dr. Holman will continue to be my guide to living on a deeper level.

Q: And what will you say to Sam?

M: I love you so much, I always want to be connected to you. The fact that I want to grow doesn't mean we will grow apart. It means I will learn to understand myself more and therefore I will be able to find those parts that are not loving; I can work at changing them to loving. And, guess what? The more I love myself, the more I will be able to love you. With you, Sam, I want to keep our passionate, erotic love. I want to be sensitive to you and your different needs, and I want you to be able to do so with me.

Q: And what will you say to Andy?

M: You're my rock and I've been your rock too. Whatever happens in life, I trust you'll be there for me and I'll be there for you. What would I do without you in my life? I love you to the depths of my heart.

Journal #1 instead of Session #23
Driving Home from Malibu

As Sam and I drove home from Malibu, I felt like an adolescent in love. I forgot that I had a child who is almost a teenager. I forgot where I live. I forgot about everything except the moments Sam and I were connected. It was glorious!

The beach house was a love nest on the Pacific Ocean, so cozy and comfortable. I don't think I could create a more tasteful and creative environment to fulfill my dreams for a getaway.

Our love has changed both of us. I can't keep my hands off of him! Lying with him is like being wrapped in a down comforter.

Who would have thought that in a year's time, such a difficult conversation could turn out so well? Driving back to town this afternoon...

S: I wish we could have stayed in Malibu forever.

M: I never experienced anything as wonderful as that in my life.

S: Would you like to spend the first nights of our honeymoon there? Spend time resting up after the wedding – before I take you to Tahiti! When would you like to have the honeymoon?

M: Well, after the wedding? (I tried to laugh and as we stopped at the light, I gave him a kiss.)

S: Molly, are you stalling?

M: Let's stop at Moonshadows again to watch the sunset.

(Once inside, settled at a table)

M: I was thinking about your question, "Am I stalling?"

S: What's on you mind?

M: Well, at the moment you asked "when," I noticed my heart skipped a beat. That's a clue to me, there's something in the back of my mind I wasn't aware of.

S: What do you think it is?

M: That's just it. I need to find out.

S: So is that a nice way of saying "No"?

M: (I took Sam's hand) Please listen... it's not about you. You're certainly enough for me. But you see how easy it is for us to misunderstand each other?

S: What am I misunderstanding? Aren't you saying "No"?

M: I could feel you pulling away. I'm so glad you're able to tell me this.

S: Well, wouldn't you?

M: Whatever it is, this sudden fear, I know it's not about you. It's a hidden barrier, something about me.

S: (Frowning) I'd like to just kick it out of the way and move on.

M: I wish you could, but we have to see it first. I need to work this out so it doesn't become a problem.

S: Do you see this barrier as interfering with our relationship or just our marriage plans?

M: I'm determined not to let that happen. That's why therapy is so important to me. I want to recognize and remove the barriers or beliefs that get in the way.

S: For example?

M: Do you remember when I made up the story that you were an alcoholic, when I found those Scotch bottles in my lingerie drawer? In hindsight, I know the problem is that I believed my story to be true.

S: How can you believe something to be true when it's not true? (He chuckled!)

M: That's just it, Sam. You put your finger right on it. How was I able to do that?

S: (Laughing) I remember I like that line from Samuel Goldwyn: "Half the lies I tell myself aren't true."

M: (Laughing too) Yes! I told myself a lie that wasn't true. It was easy. I saw the bottles at your house. I know my mother hid bottles and she was an alcoholic, so you must be an alcoholic.

S: What you're saying is you made a plausible assumption about me.

M: Right. I told myself a story. I had the proof. I felt real fear and anger so I believed it. This is my example of a barrier. I paid no attention to the fact that I'm the one who made up the story. It took hard work for me to recognize it and pay attention. I found out, as you say, "Half the lies I tell myself aren't true."

S: When it happens, you don't know if it's true or not. I wonder what hidden beliefs *I* bring to the party. (We both laughed.) I wonder what lies I tell *myself* that aren't true.

M: (I was thinking, "I'm so lucky. Imagine finding a man who's so open. He's not only interested in listening, but he turns things around and takes a look at himself. I smiled at him adoringly.)

S: (I hope he was thinking, "What a woman! She really wants us to be happy. And she's great in bed!") "Molly, you're awesome. Maybe someday I'll ask you to marry me."

What an amazing twenty-four hours we had! Back in my driveway in West L.A., Sam opened the car door for me and teasingly said, "I would love to carry you over the threshold, but first take a look." He pointed to the brilliant red still lighting up the sky. "My heart feels on fire," Sam murmured.

I left the front door half-open to feel the unseasonal tropical warmth of the Santa Anas. Sam bent down to my 5'5" level and folded me tenderly into a hug – I felt engulfed by him. I whispered into his ear, we giggled and he lightly swatted my bottom as he left.

I was ready to go pick up Sara next door and make her favorite Sunday dinner. Searching for the Sinatra CD I loved, I put it on and turned up the volume. I began to sing along with Frank as I walked outside.

When I turned on the front lawn sprinklers, the falling sunlight danced through the water. Putting my arms around myself, I stood still in the sprinklers drenching myself in the cool water, my white blouse revealing a youthful, sexual figure. I belted out "Fly Me To The Moon."

Feeling euphoric, I threw one clog into the air and shouted, "I'm in love with Sam!" I threw off the other clog and yelled out, "I'm in love with Andy!" As I whirled around, I said, "I'm still free!"

Epilogue

In the months since the earthquake, I'm realizing January17th is a night for my personal celebration. That intriguing though traumatic night marks the beginning of my sexual evolution.

While Sam was asleep in our hotel room at the Lunamare, I created so many fantasies. I nurtured them with food and drink, dressed them up, tried them on, stretched them and shrunk them according to my fancy, and through foreplay like that, I snuck up on my confused sexual self. When I awakened Sam, it was because *I* wanted sex. I love that! I was just high enough on various substances and high enough on love and romance that the lower part of my body got high too! Oh that feeling, or as Bob Seger says, "That fire down below!" To feel my body responding so acutely and then to have it so rudely interrupted by Mother Nature's version of an orgasm was at once frustrating and fascinating. Right now, I only want to dwell on what I felt in those too few minutes before it all came to an abrupt end.

My breasts looked beautiful in the shadows cast by the moonlight, my back supple, my legs long, my breath came hard and fast and full of drive – Sam bouncing off my uncharted moves, following my lead, intermittently elastic and taut, but always, I was the rider, not the horse. I was strong! So much sexual power and yet soft enough to melt at his touch. Oh my . . .

Oh
My
God!

Author Bio
Eleanor Kendall

Eleanor Kendall was born in Toronto, Canada. During World War 11 she volunteered working in Wartime Day Nursery. Later she graduated from the Institute of Child Study at the University of Toronto with a degree as a nursery school teacher. She studied under William E. Blatz, MD,PhD in psychology, who established the Institute of Child Study with a grant from the Rockefeller Foundation. Eleanor was trained by Master Teachers like Margaret Fletcher and later was herself the Master Teacher who trained many teachers for her own nursery school.

In 1948 Eleanor moved to Pacific Palisades, CA, where, with her new husband, commissioned Lloyd Wright, Architect, the eldest son of Frank Lloyd Wright to design a nursery school building which when completed was called Hill and Dale Nursery Kindergarten. Thirty years later, this school became non-profit and Eleanor started a private practice in family counseling, having already taken many courses from the Thalian Clinic. She also benefited from years of therapy with Maurice Rapkin, PhD who became Eleanor's next Master Teacher and supervised her counseling work. Work with Dr. Rapkin inspired her to write a book about Love and Anger. She organized a group of dedicated writers who took 14 years to produce a book called "Love and Anger" which would perpetuate the psychological insights from the definitive model of Anger developed by Dr. Rapkin.

Author Bio
Maurice Rapkin

Maurice was born in Woodbine, New Jersey on June 5, 1916, but lived in California most of his life. Maurice raised his son, and two daughters with his loving wife Shirley.

Maurice Rapkin received his bachelor's degree in 1938 from CCNY and his PhD in Clinical Psychology from the University of Southern California in 1949. Maurice Rapkin was a clinician's clinician. He spent most of his career developing and professionalizing the independent practice of clinical psychology. Maurice headed the first wave of University trained Clinical Psychologists to enter private practice.

Maurice was one of the founders of the Los Angeles Society of Clinical Psychologists (LASCAP) in private practice, and in 1956 became its president.

Maurice was one of the initiators of the Psychology Licensing Act in the early 1960s. He was instrumental in the development of the Psychology Certification. and he was appointed by Gov. Edmund Brown to the Psychological Examining Committee, (where he served for nine years), including one year as chairman.

Maurice described himself as an eclectic practitioner drawing upon Client Centered, Psychoanalytic, Reichian, Gestalt, Transpersonal, Transactional, and Cognitive theories and practices. He arrived at his "Hot Potato Theory of Anger" and the "Power of Pretend" as the focus of his therapy.

Maurice said "I view the central focus of therapy as helping the client to recognize the Omni-presence of his anger arising from blocked positive wishes, and to learn how to handle it constructively. The Power of Pretend focuses on the deliberate control of the fantasy process as a key element in processing anger, so that the client moves increasingly toward happy and loving self-fulfillment".

When asked "What should be the main concerns for the practice of clinical psychology?". Maurice replied "I believe that world peace begins with me. Psychologists who increasingly understand and master their inner life can make the best contribution to our community. We have techniques to help others live more loving lives. Just as theoretical physics and metaphysics are growing closer, I like to think that clinical psychologists will expand their awareness to include more and more of the knowledge available from metaphysical sources. This will make them more effective as therapists".

Previously Published Articles
by
Maurice Rapkin, Ph. D.

Anger As A Hot Potato:
Constructive Options in Handling Anger

Maurice Rapkin, gave his first workshop on the Power of Pretend, at the 1970 meeting of the American Academy of Psychotherapists. He's been developing and expanding his ideas ever since.

My explorations of ways to handle anger constructively led to the development of my HOT POTATO theory of ANGER.

The following is a brief statement of the theory. It includes:
1. Where anger comes from,
2. How we usually handle it,
3. What anger is, and
4. New ways to handle anger constructively.

The theory draws upon a mixture of the frustration-aggression hypothesis, Reichian concepts, with some new ideas particularly about the deliberate control of fantasy processes (Power of Pretend). From this blend we derive new understanding of worry, hurt, fear, hope, depression, low self-esteem, responsibility, guilt, revenge, justified anger, jealousy, forgiveness, psychosomatic reactions, etc. Also, we develop methods of bringing all of these under conscious control leading to self-trust, self-liking, ability to sustain intimate, loving relationships, pleasurable spontaneity, creativity and "ahimsa" (behavior that is non-hurtful of self or others.)

Anger comes in three forms-hot, cool and hidden. Hot Anger is disapproved of in our society, so we learn a repertoire of coping skills. We learn to shift our anger from one skill to another, like a hot potato never, however, without cost.

I. WHERE DOES ANGER COME FROM?

Anger comes primarily from the blocking or stopping of positive Impulse• Wishes. Let me call these I.W.'s, and define them by example, e.g., moving, breathing, eating, touching, sexing, loving, playing, creating, exploring, eliminating. Their common quality is that they are spontaneous, pleasurable, take place in the present, and are not hurtful of self or others. When one or more of these wishes are blocked, anger will usually ensue.

II. USUAL COPING METHODS

A. ATTACK OUT

Society (which I prefer to call the Critics Committee) often disapproves of hot anger-with one exception. If you are justified, it is OK to Attack Out. For example, "If he hits you first, you can hit him back." We are encouraged to use our intellect in the service of justifying attacking out. Blaming is a form of such justifying.

There are four modalities through which we Attack Out:

1. Physical
2. Verbal
3. Fantasy
4. Visual

Physical and verbal are self-explanatory. Fantasies (which includes day-and-night dreams) in which there is a bad outcome to someone else, are considered hidden anger. Visual anger, -e.g. "looking daggers," has been accorded considerable importance by Reichians in the structure of the personality.

B. SUPPRESS

We can be consciously angry and decide not to do anything about it.

C. ATTACK IN

As with ATTACK OUT, there are the same four modalities through which you can ATTACK IN. Physical and verbal are self-explanatory. Fantasy, where there is a bad outcome to oneself. Worry, we now understand, is a fantasied bad outcome to someone cared about (self or others). Visual, if you look at your image or parts of your body with disapproval.

A very important part of the Hot Potato theory is the following: when you ATTACK IN, you will receive signals, such as depression, guilt, sad• ness, shame, low self-esteem, embarrassment, insecurity, humiliation, etc. Once you identify these as signals, you can use the new ways to handle anger, focusing on the origin of the signals (directing anger inward) rather than on the story of guilt, or what to do about low self-esteem or sadness. More about this when we discuss the new coping methods.

The following are variations of directing anger inward. Note that the motivation here is to be in good standing with the Critics Committee.

D. MARTYR-"I will gladly (or sadly) endure ..."

E. REVERSE-"I am not angry at them, it's they who are angry at me."

F. ENLIST-Binding one's anger into a worthy or justified cause.

G. WITHDRAW-Leave the scene or pull inward.

The latter leads to the psychological feeling of "hurt," and physiologically to what Reich calls the "shrinking biopathies." Thus, I am the one who does "hurt" to myself. No one else can do it.

What someone else can do is to set up conditions under which I will decide to withdraw. The signal, I then perceive is called "hurt."

H. REPRESS-Anger is hidden from consciousness, often signaled by psychosomatic reactions (headaches, high blood pressure) or compulsive acting out.

I. IDENTIFICATION WITH THE AGGRESSOR-" I am not angry at you. I agree with you so thoroughly that we are as one."

J. ETC.-Such other skills as Accusing Silence, Placating, Role-taking (role of victim, injustice gatherer, injured innocence, etc.)

THE RESERVOIR OF ANGER

The Reservoir symbolizes a person's ability to hold anger. This reservoir is analogous to Reich's "character armor." The reservoir container has a lid, and when conditions are right, the lid will be opened and anger released. The conditions, if it is safe and/or the justification is sufficient. Paradoxically, this puts good relationships on a collision course. When your loving partner is non-threatening, it is safest to release pent-up anger. If the target partner is unaware of this underlying tendency, he may "take it personally," not recognizing that behind the attack are unfulfilled positive wishes or a wish that the partner change so that good feeling could prevail.

He may then Attack Out or direct the anger inward (probably with• draw and do "hurt"). Subsequently, the partner may put distance between you. However, if the partners understand this process, they may work

Together to release the reservoir of anger. This cooperation wards off a collision and encourages an ever-deepening relationship.

Ill. WHAT IS ANGER?

We postulate that anger has two aspects; physiological and psychological anger.

This is a state of arousal accompanying the release of adrenalin into the blood stream. It is variously called the Emergency Reaction (W.B. Cannon); the Fight/Flight reaction; the adrenalin reaction. It is a primitive reaction to perceived danger or to the blockage of impulse-wishes (I.W.). Primitive refers to the fact that all warm-blooded animals have it. In an evolutionary sense, it enhanced survival. In our civilized society, it can be beneficial or detrimental, depending upon our understanding of the process.

The Fight/Flight reaction is characterized by faster breathing, faster heart beating, the blood vessels of the viscera contract and those of the big muscles expand, the distance senses (vision, hearing, smell) become more acute, the pain threshold goes up, the blood clotting time goes down, there may be elimination from the bladder and evacuation of feces, the liver releases blood sugar into the bloodstream, the pores open to keep the person from overheating-all to enable the organism to fight harder or to run faster. The keynote is-MOVE!

PSYCHOLOGICAL ANGER

Psychological Anger refers to what we tell ourselves about the situation: both the external and internal situation. For example, if a man comes home tired and hungry after a long day's work and dinner was supposed to have been ready but wasn't, he might tell himself that his wife was lazy or inconsiderate, and that he was justified in being angry at her. (ATTACK OUT, verbal). Or, he could tell himself that since his wife usually had dinner on time, that something bad must have happened to her (ATTACK OUT, fantasy). Or, he might think, I shouldn't be tired! What is the matter with me! Maybe I'm getting old or sick. (ATTACK IN, verbal).

According to the theory, this physiological anger state arises out of unfulfilled wishes to cat and to rest. Depending on what he tells himself, his mood state might be hot anger, cool anger, or sadness, lowered self-esteem, or worry, etc. Note that this simple example deals with an I.W., that is relatively free of taboos (compared with sexing or exploring), and thus is relatively easy to resolve. But the principle is the same.

IV. NEW-FASHIONED COPING METHODS

These methods are based on the foregoing division of anger into two components: physiological and psychological. We can change our story (psychological) and we develop new ways to discharge the heightened arousal state (physiological). In the situation of the hungry man, he could tell himself that he was in an aroused state due to his unfulfilled wish to be eating. Then he could ask his wife what he could do to facilitate making the meal, and he could busy himself doing it. If he felt more aroused, he could tell himself that he had tapped into his reservoir of anger and that this called for more vigorous movement. So, he could pound his bed with a towel or tennis racket, or he could swim, skip rope or run around the block. It is important that while he is MOVING that he does not use the Old-Fashioned Coping method of blaming or justifying his anger. Rather, he should be thinking, as he runs, that he is doing good things for himself. And that after he experiences the extra adrenalin as lessened, or as pleasurable, he is then ready to go on the Treasure Hunt. The Hunt is to identify the unfulfilled impulse wish (the Treasure).

V. FACILITATIVE WISHES

In working our way back from anger toward the I.W., we usually deal with facilitative wishes (F.W.). These arc wishes, plans or actions to change the situation that would make possible the fulfillment of l.W.'s. Thus, the F.W. is an alternative to going into Anger. Example: "I wish I had more money." "I wish I were more popular." "I wish I could rest." "I wish you would love me." "I wish the meal were ready." (Alternative labels for these wishes might be "make-possible wishes," or. implementing wishes, or, planful wishes). F.W.'s may be followed by facilitative or planful actions.

Behind every complaint. there is a F.W. For example, if the complaint were. "I don't have enough money." the F.W. might be. "I wish I had more money." At first glance, the difference between these two statements may not appear to be of much consequence. However, in terms of the theory, this difference is of utmost importance. The first statement is an ATTACK IN, verbal. That person's attitude is one of pessimism and defeat. We could say that the person chooses this self-image and mobilizes his resources to carry out his self-image. On the other hand, the second statement is optimistic. The attitude is positive-expectant. The person chooses and commits to the possibility of fulfilling his F.W.'s He may then create other F.W.'s, i.e., "I will improve my skills and earn more money."

A common facilitative action is bargaining. Very young children bargain in ways that can have lasting consequences in terms of personality structure. The young child's strongest bargaining tool is his Impulse Wishes. He knows how good it feels and how important it is to the adult, so he can say, "If you don't do what I want you to do, that will make me feel good, then I won't eat." or "I won't breathe," or "I won't talk," or "I won't move my bowels."

The parent cannot use the above approach too well. His main bargaining tool is his ability to withdraw-either physically, or support of good feelings. This presents the young child with potential disaster as far as the child's IW.s are concerned. Other facilitative actions are assertion and vows. Some actions are more effective than others.

VI. CRITICS COMMITTEES

As the young child carries out his impulse wishes, he comes up against obstacles. Among these obstacles are the behavior and attitudes of other people. The child deals with these obstacles in various ways, including going into agreement with them. In this way, he creates his own Critics Committees. We found it useful to postulate two such committees. One which is opposed to the expression of anger (except when justified). The other committee disapproves of the I.W.'s. Committee members are essentially ATTACK OUTERS, most commonly using the verbal modality (TELLERS). As such, they tell you what you should or shouldn't do, without having been invited to do so. And, characteristically, they justify their Attack Out. They openly, or by implication, give you the good (plausible) reasons for telling you, and do not give the real reasons for their angry behavior (Telling). i.e. unfulfilled I.W.'s.

VII. **DEALING WITH ANGER**

A. **MY OWN ANGER**
In dealing with my own anger, I usually start with an awareness of being hot angry, cool angry or hidden angry. The new options proposed by the Hot Potato theory are: first, to identify the Old-Fashioned coping method I am using. If I am ATTACKING OUT, justifying myself, then I will change my story. I will not justify nor blame, nor enter into an agreement or disagreement with the Critics. I will ask myself what is it that I want?, or how would I like it to be? (F.W.'s or I.W.'s). Then I will take steps to accomplish it. If I am in a strong physiological anger (arousal 1 state, I will MOVE. If it is not appropriate to move, I will tremble, telling myself that's only my good ol' body taking care of itself. Essentially, I will be separating anger into its two components-Psychological and Physiological anger. When I get to the I.W.'s, I may have to deal with the Critics Committee against pleasure. When I finally do the I.W., I may feel happy, pleasured, joyful, content, self-assured, trusting, etc.

If I am ATTACKING IN (I can tell by the signals), I will either Attack Out first, and then continue on as above, or as I become more skilled, I will Identify my F.W., and then go into Facilitative action. Again, depending on the degree of adrenal reaction, I may opt to move-as did the hungry man. Finally, I will do the I.W., with pleasure.

B. **DEALING WITH CRITICS**
Internal Critics-Members of the Critics Committees are internalized. One option is to accept them as a "given" in this world. Then we handle them by trying to win their approval and avoid their disapproval (using Old• fashion coping skills). Another option (New-fashioned coping method) is to identify them as ATIACK OUTERS, and with an attitude of curiosity, explore (I.W.) with them their real

reasons for their anger. The drills and exercises to accomplish this include two-chair Gestalt dialog and spoken or unspoken Pretend constructions. In two-chair dialog, the objective is to help them get behind their anger to their F.W.'s, and then to their I.W.'s. We don't fight or argue with them. Nor do we defend ourselves. We simply turn our spotlight onto them.

An example of an unspoken Pretend construction would be to Pretend that you ATTACK OUT in whatever manner you wish, the one you are angry at. Attack until you are satisfied. Then Pretend that the target person acknowledges the truth of your justified anger. Further, he asks for forgiveness and asks what he can do to make it alright with you. Pretend that you tell him, and he does it. Pretend that you make up. Let yourself be aware of your positive body feelings. Going into the exercise, it is important that the Pretending person be fully aware that he is the sole author of the Pretend, and, as such, is entitled to have the Pretend story go exactly as he wishes. It should be clearly understood that he is dealing with Pretends, and not with external reality.

EXTERNAL CRITICS-OTHER PEOPLE'S ANGER

When other people are angry at me, my physiological state may go into an adrenal reaction. My Old-fashioned options were described previously. I could ATTACK OUT, or ATTACK IN, etc. The new-fashioned way is to listen to the angry one with curiosity and interest. I do the Impulse Wish (exploring). I observe how he might be justifying himself; or releasing from his anger reservoir. I disregard as much as I can the content of what he is saying, reminding myself that he is not saying what are his wishes for himself (behind a complaint is a wish, either I.W. or F.W. I also keep in mind that basically he is trying to change the situation in some way that will enable him to feel good. Just as with the inner Critics, I will not defend or justify myself. I will keep the attention on him. If possible, I will acknowledge that he is angry and I will ask how he would like it to be. If he follows that path, and states a facilitative wish, I will ask him to suppose that wish is fulfilled, and then what for him? When he finally states his I.W., he will be feeling good. (We know from our work with Pretending, that when one creates a good Pretend, one feels good.) That is the time to negotiate with him about the two of you. Example: In a group, a man had been making critical remarks to a woman.

Woman: (calmly) I notice that you keep taking shots at me.

Man: (tensely) I'm really angry at you for being so critical of me.

Woman: I get that you don't like it. How would you like it to be?

Man: I wish you would listen to me, to what I'm saying.

Woman: (with interest) How would it be if I listened to you?

Man: (beginning to relax) It would show me that you like me, cared about me.

Woman: And if that happened?

Man: (smiles) Oh, then I would like you, and I would let you nnow that. (I.W.)

Woman: (smiles) I must say, that sounds nice.

Naturally, this approach works better if both people understand what is going on.

C. DEALING WITH GUILT OR DEPRESSION

We mentioned earlier that ATTACKING IN is signaled by feelings such as guilt, depression, low self-esteem, shame, etc. Therapeutically, we can explore the content of the stories that accompany these feelings. Or we can go at it by changing our story. i.e.. I am feeling guilt or I am depressed because I have directed anger inward. I have done this by agreeing with a Teller or a member of the Critics Committee that I am bad or have done wrong. I no longer will agree, rather, I will view the Teller as a person who is himself angry out of un-fulfillment. I will acknowledge that what he says may sound plausible, but I will keep my full awareness upon his motive in talking to me-i.e., is he trying to justify his anger? And if I can identify the Teller, I might wonder about his I.W.'s. I will not honor his reasons by attacking them, nor will l defend myself. I will no longer attempt to be in good standing with the Critics.

My second move will be to acknowledge my aroused physiological state and decide whether I need to MOVE. Then I will go on my wn Treasure Hunt.

In general, any physical or psychological distress is a signal to go on a Treasure Hunt.

D. FEAR AND TREMBLING

The Emergency Reaction says fight or run. Human beings have another alternative which is to decide to neither fight nor run. If we tell ourselves a story which foretells a bad outcome, to us, if we move (ATTACK IN, fantasy), then we will stand still. The Physiological Anger state at this point includes tension in the muscles (Move-Don't Move), sinking feeling in the viscera (because of the contraction of the blood vessels), additional adrenalin being produced (because of the bad fantasy), and the faster heart, breathing, etc. However, the body has a device to use up the adrenalin, namely, to tremble. We can now see how we have created all the ingredients of what we call "fear" - the psychological aspect (a prediction of a bad out•come) plus the physiological aspect-tensions, sinking feeling trembling, faster heartbeat, etc.

Once again, we can handle it differently by changing our story,i.e., recognizing what was described above, abandoning the bad prediction, congratulating ourselves for the trembling mechanism, MOVING, and then on to the Treasure Hunt.

The foregoing covers the main outlines of the theory. Following are some relevant considerations that do not fit neatly into the theory presentation.

1. For a long time now, sex and its taboos have occupied a preeminent place in dynamic personality therapy. As the taboos have lessened and sexual expression becomes more acceptable, the importance of anger and its taboos has become more evident. In the HOT POTATO theory, sex is forbidden by the Critics Committee Against Pleasure. When the I.W.'s of sex are stopped (by accepting the Critics) then anger ensues. Anger. in turn, is forbidden by the Critics Committee Against Anger. If anger is directed inward, then we feel guilt, depression, low self-esteem, psychosomatic reactions, insecurity, shame, etc.

2. Justified Anger

ATTACK OUT is sanctioned provided it is justified. Under this arrangement, the intellect is enlisted in the cause of finding or creating "good reasons" to be angry, and is directed away from the real reasons. Justified anger is such a deeply ingrained aspect of our culture, that I consider it a major insight when a patient "sees through" this process. This seems to open the way to stopping blaming of others (and of self).

3. Addictive Anger

1f one feels justifiably angry, that means one is rewarded externally by the Critics Committee. One is also rewarded internally when one is in an arousal state, by the pleasure which accompanies ACTION. (i.e., the expression of anger.) However, these secondary satisfactions leave the I.W.'s unsatisfied which generates more anger. which is channeled into ATTACK• ING OUT, thus creating an addictive cycle.

4. Getting the Anger Out

Many therapeutic approaches favor getting the anger out.

In HOT POTATO terms, this is moving in the right direction, but it does not go far enough. If it stops at justified anger, the person remains locked into addictive anger. To get full benefit the patient must use his intellect as a facilitator of the I.W.'s. We suggest changing the language from "I'm angry at..." to "I'm angry out of ...." (unfulfillment of an I.W.)

5. Pretending

Pretending (fantasizing) plays a large part in anger dynamics. Most of the stories we tell ourselves (psychological anger) are Pretends. In our Power of Pretend work, we do drills and exercises to establish more deliberate controls over this creative process. Pretending is the basis for hope, worry, fear, blaming, justifying. By becoming aware of our own rules for Pretending, we can more easily authorize ourselves to change the stories we tell ourselves and move from Psychological Anger to Facilitative Wishes. Our options increase as we become aware that we are the creators of the Pretends.

6. Drills and Exercises

In this presentation, we are not able to present in detail the drills and exercises we use. Some of these are physical (based on Neo-Reichian techniques), some are verbal (based on Gestalt), some are through Pretending, and some are cognitive.

DISCUSSION

Our basic premise is that anger (hot, cool, hidden) rises out of unfulfilled positive wishes. Typically, we learn to ignore this. Instead, the Tellers encourage us to turn our attention to the problem of what to do with the hot potato (anger). Our intellect is caught up in justifying the anger, blaming and defending against blame. In the now approach, there is no blaming. We recognize anger as a signal to go on a treasure-hunt. Our intellect is now used, in non-hurtful ways, to facilitate the journey.

CONCLUSION

I believe that in the HOT POTATO Theory and techniques, there is a basis for helping individuals, families and organizations, to change from tense, competitive, low self-esteem, depressed, jealous, belligerent, life destructive attitudes, to those of cooperation, self-liking, consideration of others, life-positive happy, content. My pretend is that if this knowledge were widely known and practiced, it would have a significant effect on social and political institutions!

REFERENCES

Rapkin. M. Discovering the double pretend. Voices. 1975. II (2). 70-73.

Rapkin, M. Pretending, thinking and feeling in psychotherapy. Voices, 1974, 10, (1) 14-21.

Rapkin. M. Taking responsibility. Unpublished manuscript.

Rapkin, M. The power of pretend. D. Nolte.Ed. Privately published. 1973

A JOURNAL PUBLISHED BY THE AMERICAN ACADEMY OF
PSYCHOTHERAPISTS
SPRING 1974
THINKING/FEELING IN PSYCHOTHERAPY

Pretending, Thinking and Feeling in Psychotherapy
By
MAURICE RAPKIN

I have been "Pretending" since 1965.

I tentatively led my first workshop in the Power of Pretend at the AAP meeting in Newport Beach, California, in July 1970. Colleagues encouraged me to do more workshops. Now I feel that I have a tiger by the tail-this stuff really works as a mind-expander. It has overtaken my earlier interest-how to deal with anger constructively. I pretend I will finish the anger book soon anyway.

During my 23 years as a therapist in private practice, I have had a variety of therapeutic experiences-formal and informal-my latest is Neo-Reichian.

My main hobby is sharing growing-mostly plants and people-including myself. I lead workshops called, "The Self-creating Person," "Taking Responsibility," "Power of Pretend."

Lately, I've developed a yen for writing. This paper was one of the most exciting experiences of my exploring life-it grew me while I was growing it.

I. INTRODUCTION
Like the body-mind dichotomy, the thought-feeling pair is a mental construct. We can have fun exploring where one begins and the other leaves off.

Out of my explorations with the Power of Pretend exercises, I choose to regard these feelings as consequences of the pretending.

As for psychotherapy, I have long since regarded it as a learning process. Sometimes I tell the people I work with that I view it as having two aspects• the untying of knots, and the learning about our options to use our newly-freed or uncommitted energies. The untying of knots aspect includes the view that pretending, in children, is the vehicle through which they make the "big decisions"-those which mold their subsequent behavior. Rather than viewing infants and children as helpless and dependent, I adopt the assumption that they possess enormous power over themselves. They make decisions which can last a lifetime. And they do it so easily that it usually escapes notice. As they grow a little older, they strive to use rational thinking to "overcome" or to deny the validity of fantasy thinking. The consequences of this in psychotherapy will be discussed later.

Power of Pretend aims to free the oppressed (Pretending) and thereby the oppressor (Reasoning) so that the two can co-exist cooperatively.

How the insights gained from Power of Pretend exercises are used in the second aspect of therapy, that is, what we can do with the freed-up or uncommitted energy, is a long story. Suffice it to say that I have been meeting once a week with a group for about three years, doing Pretend exercises and exploring the consequences.

II. DESCRIPTIONS OF POWER OF PRETEND EXERCISES

The Power of Pretend exercises are a series of graduated exercises and sequences which can be done either individually or in groups. An example of a simple exercise is

Exercise 1

"Will you pretend that you are holding an apple in your hand?"

"Now, will you stop pretending that you are holding an apple in your hand?" These are easy and fun and the participants are usually eager to share their experiences. Learning takes place out of one's own direct experience. Hopefully, it does not prematurely stir up the prejudicial vigilance of "rational thinking," but rather, it encourages empirical exploration.

What could one learn from this exercise? People report different experiences, like:

"My apple was big and juicy." "Oh, my apple was a little rotten on one side." "I couldn't pretend an apple." "It was easier to pretend an apple than to stop pretending it."

Questions emerge: Who "created" the apple? -Me, or you, who asked me to do it? Why did I create a big juicy apple (or a rotten one)? How do I create it? How do I stop creating the apple?

At first, we make observations mostly about the process of Pretend with less attention paid to content or mood. Observe that we are beginning to legitimatize fantasy thinking by "taking seriously" that we can deliberately pretend an apple. That is, we are using our rational thinking to think about and make discoveries about our irrational or fantasy thinking. We notice that there are individual differences in the way people pretend. Each person becomes more aware of his own uniqueness.

In the second request, "Will you stop Pretending" we reintroduce a process that is as important and even more overlooked than pretending.

When we deliberately stop pretending the apple, we become conscious of an option that can be very important. Thus, if we should pretend a monster who is pursuing us, and we have all the body feelings, and thoughts that would support the notion that it is real, then it is very helpful to know that we can stop pretending the monster anytime we like to and even though the body feelings and emotions may persist for awhile, we "know" that the monster is not real.

By becoming aware of the lag between the thought or visual image of the monster and the "scared feelings," we can become aware that the two events are separable; and further, that by Pretending a monster we set off accompanying body feelings. And when we stop pretending deliberately, we can continue to "feel scared" for a while even though we have stopped "thinking scared." With this awareness firmly established, we can become immune to our own self-created scares. (I imagine that this covers 99.92% of our scare experiences, including being afraid of being afraid).

We begin to explore the properties of Pretending.

It is likely that if you do these exercises yourself before you read on, it will enhance the whole undertaking, And you might make some discoveries yourself.

Exercise 2.

"Would you Pretend a red apple?" "Now, would you pretend that the red apple turns green?" "Then turns yellow?" Now, would you stop Pretending the apple?"

People experience changing their mental pictures (pretends) and become aware that they themselves have done it. This is often experienced as a big surprise. "I did it!"

Exercise 3.

"Would you Pretend that you are lying in a hammock?" "Now, will you Pretend that the hammock is hung between two trees?" "Now, will you stop Pretending the trees?" "Now, will you stop Pretending the hammock?" "What did you experience?"

Sue: "When I stopped Pretending the trees, I fell down and bumped my head. I got mad at you for that."

Ted: "I didn't fall, I just hung there unsupported in the hammock. But when you took away the hammock, I fell."

Len: "I did not fall at all-I just hung there, and when I stopped Pretending the hammock, I was back here in my chair."

We observe here that people have rules about their Pretending. Sue seems to limit her Pretending out of "realistic" considerations. Len is more open to Pretend without "realistic" considerations.

Here we see an example of rational thinking (R-think) interacting with pretend thinking (P-think). The recognition of these two kinds of thinking and the interplay between them becomes for me a very useful tool for dealing with the thinking-feeling dichotomy in psychotherapy. But more about this later. I would first like to identify other discoveries about the properties of Pretend.

In discussing the experience afterward, Sue discovered that she had had the option not to Pretend a fall, but could have Pretended to float just as Len did. Thus, she discovered a rule-in Pretending, as soon as you discover a limit or a rule, you have the power or option to overcome or change it.

Sue also discovered that in the realm of Pretending, she could Pretend to fall and hurt her head, or not. She had the option.

Also, she discovered that she pretended the pain and that she then had the choice to "do" it or not. She had the option-no one else had it. She could Pretend it either way. Thus, she began to take back into her awareness the recognition of her power to bring about bodily pain; or, if she chose to, bodily comfort. She could think of herself as being justifiably angry at me for bringing her pain, or not. More important, she might be opening up to a fuller understanding of what part Pretending plays in the way she experiences pain, blame and anger.

Further, she discovered that there is a difference between "pretending" and "real." As she became acquainted with the properties of pretending, she became increasingly capable of distinguishing between the realm of "pretend" and the realm of "real." (I count this as one of the most significant goals of psychotherapy.) Ted's response illustrates another point." When you took away the hammock. "He attributed his creative image to me. (What implications does this have for his view of self in interpersonal relations?)

In the discussion which followed the exercises, where the group sanctioned pretending, Ted found it much easier for him to acknowledge that he took away the hammock. He speculated that he made that decision out of a wish to conform, or out of a wish to experience and learn. (This awareness of who does what to whom in the communication process is also a major goal of psychotherapy.)

Often in psychotherapy, when a person is confronted with the awareness that it is indeed he who is responsible, it is experienced as a shifting of blame, "It's not your fault, it's mine. "Whereas, in the Power of Pretend context, when Ted recognized what happened, he welcomed the insight. He took the power back into his own hands.

The simple Pretend exercises become more varied. There are complex Pretends and compound Pretends. Then there are sequences somewhat like Directed Daydreams, where attention is paid to content and process and mood.

We gradually become more familiar with the properties of Pretending. "There seems to be no limit to what you can Pretend." "Yes, there are limits? But what are they?" "As soon as you identify a limit, you can transcend it-and then where does it end?" "When you Pretend good, you feel good!" "When you Pretend bad, you feel bad!" "Does that mean I can control my moods? Is this a good thing to do- I mean, is it cricket?" "What is the difference between a Pretend and what is real?" "Maybe everything is a Pretend?"

The person doing the exercises and sequences begins to draw parallels between these contrived experiences wherein there is no doubt about his authorship of the Pretend, and his own spontaneous on-going Pretends in life situations. A simple example: In an exercise, a woman was riding on a cloud that was carrying her higher and higher-15,000 feet, 20,000, 30,000, 40,000 feet up. She reported later that the higher she Pretended she was, the more lonely she became. Finally, the loneliness was almost intolerable. It suddenly dawned on her that she was the one who was creating the loneliness via Pretending. She was flooded with relief and with awareness that she had experienced this loneliness feeling most of her life. Now she had a handle to it. All she had to do was to stop Pretending lonely and she stopped feeling lonely.

Some of the on-going Pretends, once recognized, give way easily, as with the previous example. Most of them, however, are enmeshed in a network of interlocking Pretends with the accompanying affects, and require much attention before they resolve.

III. POWER OF PRETEND IN THERAPY

Jerry came to therapy reluctantly. He and Laura had a previous experience in therapy which left him feeling misunderstood, criticized and unoptimistic. This was a last-ditch attempt to save the marriage.

At a week-end Power of Pretend workshop, he listened as the participants reported what they thought and felt while doing the exercises. Observing that no one criticized them, he began tentatively to talk about his own experiences.

In the therapy session Laura was very critical of his overweight problem. She, too, had been overweight and when she shed the extra pounds, she began to feel her sensuality fully. She wanted Jerry to join her. She pleaded, cajoled, seduced, threatened. No effect! In therapy we used the Pretend approach.

Therapist: "What are your Pretends about how girls regard your weight?"

Jerry: "I think they do not like my shape. They think I'm grotesque."

Therapist: :Would you pretend that you have lost weight?"

Jerry: O.K.

Therapist: "What do you Pretend will happen now?"

Jerry: I will approach the attractive girls. (pause) This time they turn me down because basically they think I'm no good. It was not really my appearance. That will be hard to take. I would rather be fat!"

Therapist: "What is the story they are Pretending about you? About your being no good?"

Jerry: "It's because of the dirty, sexy fantasies I have about them."

Therapist; "Do you perhaps have similar fantasies about your wife?"

Jerry: "Of course!"

Therapist: "And that she would be put off if she knew this?"

Jerry: "Sure, Look how she acts!"

Therapist: "Would you be willing to ask her how she feels about this?"

Jerry: (dubiously) "How do you feel, Laura?"

Laura: "Oh, I think that's so exciting I never suspected that you had those thoughts."

Jerry: (encouraged) "Sure, why do you think I come home so grumpy? I fantasize making love to you right in the living room. Then I pretend you'll be disgusted with me. So by the time I come home, I'm all grumpy-and when you approach me, it's too late! I've lost interest."

Laura: (smiling) "Try me."

The next week was the sexiest they had ever spent together, ss you might predict (pretend). In the second week following, Jerry began to find reasons not to be sexy with his wife. Which gives us a chance to do some theorizing.

THEORY

Out of the POWER of PRETEND exercises, comes an awareness of some new categories.

1. P-think-Pretend thinking. By deliberately Pretending and stop-Pretending, one can bring about moods, emotions and body sensations. Thus, in the P-think, we have the handle to the creation and modification of feelings (moods, emotions, sensations). Most of the time, this relationship goes on unnoticed by R-think.

2. R-think-Rational (or Reality) thinking. The ability to recognize and order sensory inputs. To manipulate concepts. May be used for suppressing or discrediting P-think.

3. P-feel-Feelings that arise from Pretending. Example, the feelings that occur when you think (P-think) about being with someone you care about. In therapy, P-feel includes transference reactions. Also anger, shame, guilt, embarrassment, low self-esteem, fear, worry, hope, regret. And in the body area, trembling, fight/flight body reactions, tension, headache, fatigue, restlessness, etc.

4. R-feel-Feelings that arise based on reality situations. Example, The feelings that occur when someone you care about walks into the room. In therapy this is exemplified by here-and-now reactions like rapport, irritation, enthusiasm about changes occurring, etc.

Beside the above four categories, two other categories have been identified, but remain to be explored more fully.

5. P-about-P-Pretending about Pretending. This is a form of Complex Pretending. Example: You can make a vow (P-think) and then pretend that you forgot all about it.

6. PP-Double Pretending. Or, Pretending that you are not Pretending. Or, Pretending that your Pretend is Real. This is Compound Pretend. Both Complex and Compound Pretending are involved in how a person creates his own reality.

In place of the thinking-feeling dichotomy, we now have six categories with which to R-think.

For those readers who have not experienced the Power of Pretend exercises, perhaps it would be more useful to confine ourselves to the first four categories as tools for thinking about thinking-and-feeling in psychotherapy.

We might say that much of the process in therapy consists of encouraging the person to stop distrusting his fantasies (P-think), and to share them with his therapist. The therapist, in turn, acts as if these fantasies are legitimate entities (R-think). They then jointly try to translate them into "acceptable" R-think with accompanying R-feel.

The key bottleneck is between P-think and R-think. This channel can be opened up indirectly (by listening. by reflecting feeling, by interpretations); more directly (by here-and-now confrontation or interaction); and directly (by working openly with P-think).

With Jerry, I pictured him as trying to untie his knots but not knowing how he tied them. In the Pretend Workshop he began to acknowledge the existence and nature of pretending. In the therapy hour when I asked him about his Pretends, we were admittedly communicating at the R-think level. He was searching out his Pretend, not with an attitude of doing what the therapist wanted of him, not shamefacedly revealing his "secrets," but with an attitude of responsibility• i.e., this is his power, his decision. his creation (the Pretends). With this same attitude, he recognized his self-fulfilling negative prophecy (P-think) about his wife. Then he knowingly entered into an exploration of his sexual fantasies with her.

In the second week, difficulties set in for Jerry. The realignment between R-think and P-think is not easy, because of PP and P-about-P. (Compound and Complex Pretends)

The degree to which a person is open to R-feel may be limited by P-feel commitments. For example, transference feelings may pre-empt awareness of realistic feelings toward the therapist. As Pretending comes to be understood by R-think, there is a lessening of P-think and P-feel and thereby more room for R-feel and R-think.

The foregoing paragraph may be a description of what happens in "successful" therapy. This leads me to try to formulate a list of desirable outcomes of therapy. But first let me give another example of the application of this approach to therapy.

A woman came to see me because of her distress about her marital situation. She had fallen in love with another man and her marriage of twelve years was in jeopardy. She liked her husband and was burdened by his extreme distress when she told him about it.

There may be more of such categories; for example, the R-think may turn out to be two categories, thinking, the ability to manipulate symbols. It is not concerned with the accuracy of its assumptions. 2. Realistic thinking, the ability to order sense perceptions and size up situations accurately. Realistic thinking may, at its best, turn out to be what occurs when a person has full control of P-thinking and its related P-feelings.

Ten days later, her husband phoned for a consultation. He wanted to know what was going on. In a long session, he described his sleepless nights, loss of appetite, extreme fatigue, inability to concentrate, fear of the loss of his family (wife and children) -his world had fallen apart.

I asked him how he felt and he responded that he felt deeply hurt, bewildered, helpless, destroyed. He was at a complete loss to know what to do about changing his wife's attitudes which he felt he desperately needed to do in order to get back into equilibrium.

I then asked him how he would like her to behave (P-think). He began to describe some of the good times they had had together. He was the head of the house and he prided himself in being a good husband, father and provider. He pictured his wife as being warm, appreciative, loving, giving up the other man and restoring the family circle.

I now asked him how he felt. He said, smiling, "I feel great! I'm relaxed and excited too!"

I pointed out that in the two hours that we were together, that his wife did not know anything about what was going on in him, what he said or felt. As far as he knew, she had not changed in any respect during these two hours. He, on the other hand, had experienced extreme distress and, in a matter of minutes, changed to good feelings.

At first, he was puzzled. "You mean I did it all myself? Of course I did! You mean the way I feel is under my own control? Of course it is! Boy, when can I see you again? We have a lot of work to do!"

I pictured him as a person who, through his Pretends, was creating great distress. Try as he might rationally to figure out what was wrong and how to correct it, he was not able to. That is, he thought the source of his trouble was his wife's behavior-that is what made him feel bad. Logically, then, to feel better, she would have to change. Since R-think did not acknowledge P-think, he could not look there to remedy the situation. However, as he came to acknowledge his Pretends, he opened up a direct line between his R-think and his emotions (P-feel).

To state it from the feeling side, he was a victim of his "spontaneous bad feelings," '(victim" in the sense that he was drawn into making decisions about these "real" feelings. When he was able to distinguish between P-feel and R-feel, he was able to begin to stop the P-think that evoked the P-feel (depression and elation) and to clear the way for experiencing R-feel.

(This theorizing that I have presented so 'far is admittedly sketchy. I commend it to you as possible tools for further exploration.

V. DESIREABLE LEARNING AND OUTCOMES OF PSYCHOTHERAPY

The following list is derived from experiences with Power of Pretend exercises.

1. The recognition that moods, emotion and body sensations can be elicited and controlled by Pretending. The option to feel good or bad resides in oneself. One becomes self-responsible.

2. The ability to recognize quickly the difference between "Pretend" and Real.

3. To learn the "rules" of "Pretend" and of "Real," and the ability to use these "rules" in their appropriate realm.

4. The ability to recognize other people's Pretends and to be able to choose whether or not you wish to enter into them.

4-5 Conversely, the ability to recognize and share other people's Reality.

5. To understand the properties of thinking (P-think) (R-think) and feeling (P-feel, R-feel); how they interact and their consequences. A possible model for the well-adjusted person in this area is to function primarily in the R-think. R-feel state; that is, a person who is able to think without interference from Pretending, and whose emotional responses are based on here-and-now realism without any admixture of P-feel.

If a person wished to grow into a more advanced state, he should be able to function at option in all six categories-P-think, R-think, P-feel, R-feel, P-about• P, PP.

WRAP-UP

In the background of our conscious thinking is the world of fantasy. Traditionally in therapy we bring a particular bit of it into "figure" to study its content. In the Power of Pretend exercises, we deliberately bring into "figure" the entire web work of the fantasy process.

We learn that pretending is the handle to feelings. That there is a constant, unnecessary war between pretending and rational thinking. We discover that there are "rules" of pretending that are quite different from the rules of "Real" and that when these are distinguished one from the other peace can be established. Then each one functions better and contributes to the total well-being.

We explore further and discover complex and compound Pretends. These open up for our study how we "do" repression; how we "do" belief; how we "do" reality; how we can "do" other levels of consciousness.

The more we learn about deliberate Pretend, the more we learn about spontaneous Pretend. And the more we learn about Pretend, the more we under• stand about what is Real. Many of the transactions that occur in therapy can be understood in a different way when held up to a grid of the four categories of thinking (P-think. R-think, P-about-P, PP) and two categories of feeling (P-feel, R-feel) presented here. Of particular importance is the bottleneck between R-think and P-think. D

IS "JUSTIFIED ANGER"
AN EVASION OF REALITY?
AN ESSAY ON ADDICTIVE ANGER
by
MAURICE RAPKIN Ph.D.

In this paper, I would like to examine the proposition that justified anger is all evasion of reality, as contrasted with the idea that justified anger is an accurate description of reality. It is my idea that by seeing justified anger as an evasion, we might then attend to the reality that was evaded; and, hopefully find better solutions to the problem of our ever-increasing anger, violence and destructiveness.

Secondarily. I would like to look at the negative qualities of justified anger. I came upon the notion of anger as an addictive response, by looking at a diagram of the Hot Potato Theory of Anger (Rapkin. 1977). I had an *aha!* reaction: "Justified anger is addictive." I wondered why I hadn't noticed it before.

It struck me as a potentially very fruitful concept. in the same class as Hans Selye's *aha!*, "All the patients in the hospital are sick, no matter what their diagnosis.' (Selye. 1956) Selye's discovery led to his momentous formulations about stress. I'm very curious about what the insight, "justified anger is addictive" can lead to.

To begin with, I will briefly describe the explanatory system I developed about anger, the Hot Potato Theory, as a background for the discussion of justified anger and addictive anger. While acting as a trainer in a Sensitivity Training program, I noticed how easily many of the fifteen strangers became angry at each other. It gradually became clear that behind their anger was a wish that the other person change. Further, in a layer below that wish, was an impulse to be friendly, loving and playful. It looked like this: WISHES that are blocked give rise to Anger.

The two layers of wishes I called Impulse Wishes (I.W., for short) and Facilitative Wishes (F.W.). In the group we tried to define impulse wishes by example and discovered sub-groupings: biological impulse wishes (moving, breathing, eating, eliminating, resting, sexing) and social impulse wishes (loving, playing, socializing), and solo impulse wishes (creating, exploring, completing, inner sensing).

Facilitative Wishes (F.W.s) were characterized by thinking, planning and actions whose motive was to remove the barrier to the fulfillment of the impulse wishes. For example, in the Sensitivity group I observed that John was attacking Nancy, and I asked him what he wanted from her.

He answered that he wanted her not to put him down. To me, she did not seem to be doing this. He said he wanted her to be nice to him. (Later, we labelled these Facilitative Wishes). Realizing that this was not his complete story, I asked him how it would be if his wishes were fulfilled. He thought a moment, then said, If his wishes were fulfilled, he would be friendly and playful with her. His answer surprised them both. He discovered that he had been attracted to her from the very beginning.

By looking behind his anger at Nancy, John became aware of his facilitative wish that Nancy change from down-putting to being nice. Evidently he perceived down-putting as a barrier to his own impulses to be friendly. When the barrier was identified, he then had the option to go beyond it and discovered his impulse Wishes, to be friendly and playful with her. This case very simply illustrates the movement from anger, back to its origin.

That transition, from anger back to its origin seemed easy. Then I wondered, why don't we do it all the time? I noticed that at the very beginning of the Sensitivity session, people were cautious, exploratory, polite. As time went on, some people became more silent. We speculated that there were un-stated societal attitudes about anger, namely, that to express it is not nice. But what about those who were doing it? We noticed that they would justify their anger. Somehow, Justifying seemed to make it easier for them to express their anger. But why?

I theorized that once a person showed anger, societal critics would sit in judgment. If you can justify your anger, it is o.k. to Attack Out. If you cannot, then you do something else with it. These societal critics are internalized. I refer to them as the Critics Committee.

I now thought of Anger as being like a hot potato, an uncomfortable feeling that one had to handle, either by holding onto it, or attacking someone else with it. We identified about ten other methods that people developed to handle the Hot Potato of Anger, and still remain in good standing with the Critics. The most popular of these was to direct the anger inward (Attack In). We found that we could describe anger as being hot anger, cool anger, or hidden anger. For the purposes of this paper, I want to focus on Attack Out and Attack In.

Most people's internalized Critics Committee have a rule, that it is OK to attack out, only if you are justified. They communicate their view in many ways. "If he hits you first, it is OK to hit him back". Who is to blame? "Punish the one whose fault it is etc." Thus, if you can justify your anger, such as plausibly blaming someone else, then you are in good standing with your Critics Committee when you Attack out.

Notice what has happened so far in the Sensitivity Group. John is attracted to Nancy. For reasons unknown at the time, he did not express his positive feelings. As a result, in accordance with the Hot Potato Theory, he experienced anger, and manifested his anger by criticizing Nancy. In order to placate his Critics Committee, he used his intellect to construct a justification for his anger, i.e. "She is putting me down". Then he criticized her for interrupting him, for being caught up in the Women's Lib movement, etc. Notice that John shifted his attention from the desire to experience playing and loving with Nancy, to winning the support of his critics.

From this simple case, I began to observe that changing the focus from a positive impulse wish to getting along with the CRITICS COMMITTEE was not the exception, but the rule. I noticed that blaming, justifying one's own anger, criticizing, playing the I am right, you are wrong game, was going on all over. I came to think of these as instances of changing one's attention from the pursuit of impulse wishes, to the handling of the Hot Potato of Anger. It made me wonder why if experiencing Impulse wishes was so pleasurable, why didn't people remain focused on fulfilling these, instead of spending their time and effort in accommodating the Critics? As I thought, I had an *Aha!*

JUSTIFIED ANGER IS ADDICTIVE: ..

Let's look at the definition of addiction, then at the nature of anger, and then at the Critics Committee.

Addiction: I think of an Addiction as repetitive behavior that provides some gratification Additionally, it is a substitute for other behavior which is potentially more rewarding, but is either prohibited or more difficult to do.

Anger has two components: a physiological one and a psychological one. Physiological: When a person "feels angry" or feels endangered, an extra supply of adrenalin has been released into the blood stream. This is usually experienced as a state of arousal: faster heartbeat, faster breathing; all the characteristics of the fight/flight reaction described originally by Walter B. Cannon (Cannon, 1920). This is the physiological component of anger. Reichian theory points out that if one withholds energy flow, one experiences discomfort (Reich, 1960). For example, if one feels like laughing and holds it back, one will feel uncomfortable. On the other hand, energy that flows freely through appropriate channels is experienced as pleasant, laughing, sneezing, sexual orgasm.

The psychological component of anger is the story you tell yourself about the situation. John was telling himself that Nancy was putting him down. Thus, he was justified in the eyes of his Critics in being angry at her because he perceived her as attacking him first.

Critics Committee: This "committee" is composed of the memories of the voices-and attitudes of those people in John's life who judged him: the praisers, the blamers, the advice givers; parents, teachers, siblings. peers, or even fictional characters.(as in the movies).

Now let us return to the notion of addictive anger. One of the characteristics of an addiction is that it yields some pleasure. In Justified Anger there are 3 sources of pleasure.

1. Being approved by the Critics,
2. The pleasure of the energy flow
3. The sense of thinking right.
4. Right.

If you have been in a situation where you felt safe to fully express righteous anger, then you know what a unifying experience it can be. There is a sense of wholeness, at-oneness. This, then, is the reward for attacking out.

There is another force that contributes to the addictive cycle. There is a Critics Committee that disapproves of all innocent (impulse) wishes. These critics are like the biblical angels with flaming swords that stand guard at the gates of Eden, to prevent humans from reentering the place of unlimited, innocent pleasure. Therefore, electing to be justifiably angry protects the addict from a confrontation with these formidable entities.

What about the penalties? The first penalty may be that the target of your anger will take what you say personally, then counter-attack or Attack In (withdraw). The two of you may reach a guarded truce. The second penalty is that you do not get to experience the original impulse wish, since you have shifted your attention to the anger. Furthermore, the lack of fulfillment of this wish, gives rise to additional anger, which in turn, may feed into the addictive cycle. John was unaware of this loss. Rather, he felt more at home in his justified addictive anger. The addictive anger substitutes for the impulse wish.

What happened when this process was called to his attention and he was helped to become aware that he had the impulse wishes of playing and loving with Nancy.

In this case, since Nancy was also attracted to John and said so (thereby fulfilling his facilitative wish, he freely chose to express his friendliness to her. I do not know how well he was able to sustain this change, since the training lasted just a few weeks, and we did not focus much on this issue during the training. Many people skilled in justified anger would have trouble making a change back to the source of the anger- i.e. the un•fulfilled impulse wishes. Later on, we called this transition from anger to facilitative wish to impulse wish "going on the treasure hunt"; the treasure, of course, being the impulse wishes. The model provides a basis for a person who experiences anger to ask himself, "What do I really want?" (What is my impulse wish?)

Following is an example of a woman with whom I had discussed the Hot Potato theory, at length and who was able to use it.

She reported that she returned home from an unsuccessful shopping trip late one afternoon, hot, tired and hungry. She found her teenagers in a thoroughly messed-up kitchen. She pictured herself first having to clean up the mess and then having to prepare the dinner. She felt a surge of "justifiable anger" and opened her mouth to give forth. Instead, she said to them, "just a minute, I'll be right back." She went into her bedroom and pounded on her bed until she felt released. Then she returned to the kitchen and asked the youngsters what had happened. They explained that they planned to surprise her by preparing dinner. She felt a flow of warmth and embraced them. She then took a shower and rested while they finished the preparation of the meal.

What she was able to do was to choose to keep her eye on what her impulse wishes were: eating, resting, loving. Even though her first move was into justified anger, she was able to change the stories she told herself. She then redirected her extra shot of energy into neutral release and followed that by facilitative actions; i.e., asking her children what had happened. Their response opened the way to her treasures, her impulse wishes.

It's easy to imagine the negative consequences if she had chosen to justify her anger and Attack Out.

She later reported further positive results, namely, that the teenagers began to use the same methods when they became angry.

One possibility we must consider is that this woman repressed some or much of her anger. Let's go back to the Anger theory for a moment. One of the skills of coping with the Hot Potato Theory of Anger is to hold it in what we called Attack In. Just as we came to recognize that blaming, and justifying were signals of Attack Out, we have come to recognize the signals that accompany Attack In. There may be tension, trembling, sadness and depression, lowered self-esteem, guilt, humiliation, embarrassment, fear or anxiety, helplessness, or feeling victimized. One may create stories or fantasies with bad outcomes. One may be self-critical or regretful. According to the theory, what led us to these states was the decision to handle anger in such a way as to be in good standing with the Critics Committee. In these states, an awareness of the origin of the anger seems remote.

The remedy for these symptoms is to change one's stories and to begin to turn the energy outward. However, if the energy is directed into justified anger, there is the danger of being caught in the addictive cycle. Two examples, one at the individual level, one at the societal level.

1. At one time, in therapy it was fashionable to encourage patients to get in touch with and express their anger that they felt at their parents or other hated individuals. Sometimes they were encouraged to confront that person directly. They would come away from the encounter justifiably angry at their target and might remain partially or completely estranged.

What they did not face was the reality that their anger came out of their own lack of fulfillment of impulse wishes, and as adults they could do something about that.

2. What has been happening to some segments of society such as women or African American people is that starting from an attitude of low self-esteem (Attack n), they begin to change their story to one which gives a better picture of themselves: "Women would make better political leaders, less likely to go to war, because they are more humane and closer to nature. "Or. "Black is beautiful." Instead of continuing with "White is beautiful; too, and "Let's us more humane women work with the more bellicose men." to find constructive solutions these minorities turn to Attacking Out: "Male Chauvinist Pig," and "Get Whitey". These positions are justified by generalized statements such as "Look what you have done to us for hundreds of years."

In these examples we see the addictive cycle manifested, Bolstered by their justifications and approved of by societal critics. They Attack Out. And so they remain on the Anger side. They may think they are facing reality, based on the evidence of their emotionality (which is real), and the approval of the critics, which may be remembered or current), and the pattern of their thoughts (which are plausible but inaccurate, e.g. I have not been oppressing anyone, let alone for hundreds of years.

From the point of view of the Hot Potato Theory, they are evading reality. The reality is that the signals of arousal are indicators to first express the extra energy in neutral or constructive ways, then to go on to their treasure hunt, guided by the questions. "What pleasurable impulse wishes do I have that I am not acting upon? What would make it possible for me to do so?

What commitments do I have, (like to the Critic Committees) that stand in the way?

Is it more satisfying for me to complain and criticize, as John did to Nancy, or to find out what I am not doing that I want to be doing?

It follows from the foregoing that Anger is o.k. Justified anger is something else again. Anger is ok when it is identified as a state of heightened energy and when that energy is directed toward the treasure hunt • searching out the natural wish and taking steps to remove the barriers to its fulfillment.

Justifying your anger calls for the intellect to find a good reason to satisfy your societal critics. The phrase "irrational anger" suggests that anger should be rational. In order to be in good standing with the critics, one must discover a rational explanation for the anger. As one does this, one automatically endorses the societal critics, which is counter-productive, and one turns away from the real reason for the anger: The lack of fulfillment of the natural wish.

Consider a hypothetical situation, in which a 12-year-old-neighbor deliberately throws a brick through your window. Is this an appropriate time for justified anger? To answer this, you must define your objectives. What do you want to achieve? In the light of the previous discussion about the rewards for justifiable anger, this would be a good time. Everything is favorable. The attack on you was unjustified. The boy is small, so it is safe. Almost everyone would agree with your reasons.

A second objective might be to protect yourself from a repetition of such an attack. What is the best way to do that? Call the police? Talk to his parents? Get him into therapy? Ask him why he did it? Attack the boy verbally or physically? (One could do this in unjustifiable anger or in a deliberate show of force - either way conceivably could deter him from repeating this act). Ideally, one should be able to make a conscious choice in handling the hot potato from among the old or new skills, without trying to be in good standing with the Critics Committee.

A third objective might be to get at the source of the boy's Attack Out, hopefully so that he would change from being a danger in your environment to a friend, possibly one with whom you could share impulse wishes.

A real-life experience that exemplifies the searching out of the impulse wishes occurred to a colleague.

Elizabeth is an attractive woman in her fifties who was abducted from an air terminal parking lot by a young minority man. He took her to a house where he and his friends, in the presence of their women, gang-raped her and beat her severely. The ordeal lasted many hours. Then the young man was told to take her out and kill her. On the way, stopping for a red traffic signal, he was questioned by police who discovered a near-dead Elizabeth on the floor of the back seat. She was hospitalized for many months. During that time the attacking group, who had her purse and keys, burglarized her house. For a long time she had difficulty in speaking with people, not knowing which words would come out, so she ost her teaching job at the university. She also lost her savings to medical bills, her house for failure to pay taxes, her health, and her relationship with her fiancé.

When the young man was brought to trial, Elizabeth was called as a witness. The accused man's friends and family packed the courtroom and communicated threats to her by whispers and gestures. She was advised to move and change her identity to protect herself against the time when he would be released from prison. For a long while, if she would ever see a member of that minority group at a distance, she would tremble uncontrollably with fear.

In the course of time, that fear reaction turned into hatred. She fantasized revenge of various kinds. There was no doubt about her feeling justified in the extreme retaliations she created in her mind for all those who had broken into her life.

At one point in our discussing her situation, I shared with her my view that at this minute she could consider the experience either as a tragedy or as an opportunity. As a tragedy, she could view herself as a victim and carry on her justifiable rage and fear. As an opportunity... Well, she gradually began to think about her assailant and his motives. She wondered what his upbringing must have been like. Perhaps other rapists were exposed, as little boys, to attitudes that were similar. She began to think of ways to help them, such as a Rape Hot Line. She started classes about rape in an experimental college. In these classes she dealt with what to do in a rape situation, and also with the broader background from which rape behavior grew. She began to contact people to see what could be done to improve the ways the police and hospitals handled rape victims. She spoke with state legislators about improving the law which compensates innocent victims of violent crimes. She told her story on television in an effort to stimulate constructive thinking about the entire context in which the event occurred (Duncan, 1976). The television documentary won an award, and she was encouraged to write a book about it. (Duncan, in preparation). As she continues with her facilitative wish actions, she is meeting new people and her health is steadily improving; her phobic reaction is gone, her self-esteem is high, and her outlook is optimistic. She reports that the shift from justified rage to constructive actions has opened her up to a new, creative life.

Let us consider how much Attacking Out is going on in the world: individual physical violence, institutional violence (cut-throat competition, war), verbal attacking-out (complaining, name-calling, advice-giving, sarcasm, criticism. belittling); attacking out in fantasy via day dreams or night dreams that have bad outcomes to others. And consider how much Attacking In is going on, as signaled by guilt, worry, tension, fear, low self-esteem, physical illness, and mistreatment of one's body. Consider how effective or ineffective our remedial measures or preventative measures have been. To what extent have some promising measures been sidetracked into justified anger which becomes addictive? Consider too, what might happen if we used our intellect, not in the service of justifying anger or placing blame, but rather in the service of realistically viewing anger in all its forms as a signal to go on the treasure hunt. And what if we had many socially-approved measures for doing the treasure hunt as did the mother of the teenager who came home to her dirty kitchen and ended up with a wonderful meal!

REFERENCES

CANNON, Walter B., *Bodily Changes in Pain, Hunger, Fear, and Rage.* New York: D. Appleton and Company, 1920.

DUNCAN, Elizabeth, "Rape, the Hidden Crime." Don Silverman Blue Grass Productions, ABC-TV October 10, 1976

DUNCAN, Elizabeth, *When The Bough Breaks.* Manuscript in preparation

RAPKIN, Maurice, "Anger as a Hot Potato; Constructive Options in Handling Anger", *Voices: 1. American Academy of Psychotherapists,* Summer 1977, Vol. 7 No. 2, pp. 67-74.

REICH, Wilhelm, *Selected Writings.* New York: Farrar, Straus & Giraux, 1960.

SELYE, Hans, *The Stress of Life.* McGraw-Hill. New York McGraw-Hill, 1956

P A R — PRETEND ANGER RELEASE

This method of releasing anger in a safe way derives from the Anger Is A Hot Potato theory and The Power of Pretend developed by Maurice Rapkin, Ph.D.

The Narrator invites the person to find a relaxed position, and explains that the PAR is usually done with the eyes closed and without speaking. If the person feels moved to speak, that is okay.

The Narrator further explains that he will instruct the person in the process step-by-step, and to let the Narrator know when each step is completed. He tells the person that what happens will take place altogether within the person, and since all the events that will be pretended will be using the person's own energy, it is specifically agreed that no one or no thing outside of the person will in any way be harmed by what takes place.

And since the inner drama will belong entirely to the person, he or she should give himself full permission to express himself in any way he chooses. It's as if the person is the author of a story that no one else will ever read, and so he can write it in any way he wishes, recognizing that the more fully he expresses himself, the more benefit he will obtain, and that no one will be hurt by it. The idea is to allow the expression, rather than push it. When the Narrator believes that the person understands these conditions, proceed with Step 1.

STEP 1.

Let yourself remember an event in which you felt angry or irritated. Allow yourself full recall -- the person or people involved, what they were doing, saying, thinking, how they are dressed, where the event took place, the time of day, the weather and temperature, how you are dressed, what you were thinking, feeling and doing. Is the memory clear and full?

Let yourself be aware of the feelings in your body. Let yourself be aware of your angry bodily impulses to speak, yell or do. In your imagery, allow yourself to give into and express whatever anger, rage or irritation you feel. Remember, this memory is all your energy, and you have full right to do with it as your impulses dictate.

Let me know when you have expressed yourself to your complete satisfaction. Let yourself be fully aware of your body sensations. (pause) (When the person indicates, go to Step 2,)

STEP 2,

Now, have the target of your anger say to you, "Joe, (or Joan), you are absolutely right in doing or saying what you did to me." (pause) Notice how your body feels when your target says that.

STEP 3.

Now have the target person say, "Joe (or Joan), since I caused you all of this upset, what can I do to make it up to you?"

Notice what happens in your body feelings when he or she says that. If you can think of something he can do, tell him, and let him do it. Then notice how you feel. (pause) If you couldn't or didn't want to tell him, it suggests that you still have some anger toward him. Go back to STEP 1. and express that. Then STEP 2. and 3. (pause)

STEP 4.

When he has performed the make-up act, do you feel okay about forgiving him?

Can you embrace him? If so, do.

How does that feel? (If it feels good) stay with that feeling; enjoy it for a moment or two.

If the person does not wish to forgive or embrace, you might suggest that he tries it on for size, and if it still does not feel good, that suggests that there may be residual anger. If appropriate, repeat STEPS 1 – 4.

COMMENT

People familiar with the "HOT POTATO THEORY OF ANGER" will recognize that the PAR is dealing in an OLD-FASHIONED way with JUSTIFIED ANGER. The inner experience of forgiving and embracing may or may not help the person get back to his original Impulse Wishes.

After the person becomes familiar with the STEPS 1 - 4, he can do the process by himself,

One person reported that he found it effective in getting a good night's sleep, to examine his feeling state when he lay down to sleep to see if he was aware of any anger or irritation. If so, he ran PARs until they were gone.

Another person liked playing the target when he acknowledged responsibility for causing the person's upset, and asking what he could do to make it up. He tried it in his relations with other people and it worked well for him.

Gems

By blaming someone else, you give your power to them to fix it, and until they do what you want, you'll feel frustrated and unhappy.

It feels so good to feel good, why don't we do it all the time?

Holman says: Feeling sad is a clue that you are holding anger in.

Depression has been taken over by the pharmaceutical companies.

"The Great I Don't Know" is the key to opening doors that were locked by inaccurate assumptions.

In school, if you don't know, you are in trouble. In real life, when you really don't know, and you use "The Great I Don't Know", it opens up the world to be explored.

Judge not lest ye become a judge.

Half the lies I tell myself aren't true.

About taking things personally;
All events are neutral.
We are the ones who give them color and meaning.

Often when a person says I can't, they mean I won't,
unless, or until my conditions are met.

Going into a new relationship, if you don't understand why the old one did not work out, you will use the same coping methods that you already know, with the same probable outcome.

Good Relationships are on a Collision Course

Loving relationships provide an opportunity for each person to grow. However, because each person brings to the relationship a collection of unfinished business, the lovers are on a collision course. Sometimes these collisions happen early, like in lover's quarrels. But whether it's sooner or later, these unfinished businesses, can either minimize or destroy the relationship. All is not lost. There is another choice. In therapy, each person can reopen their unfinished business and then complete it. That means rediscovering the anger and the positive feelings that were blocked. This releases each lover to grow and become more spontaneous and fun-loving, contributing stimulation and joyfulness to the relationship. No collision?

How do you know you have unfinished business? Following are a few clues; fears, keeping secrets, having demanding expectations, ambitiousness, hurts, feeling of being less than, fear that the other shoe will drop, competitiveness, approval seeking, mind reading, stress and tension, depression, envy, jealousy and being accident prone.

When you run out of these clues, there are many more, like in ability to tolerate pleasure, fear of death, fear of success, not to mention psychosomatic illness. Just imagine how much pleasurable fulfillment can lie behind these states of mind and body. Buried treasure!

The Platinum Rule

Do unto yourself as you would have others do unto you.

This came to me in a dream. Then I asked, "Won't people say I'm selfish?"

What we mean, they explained was to be as caring, attentive, thoughtful and loving of yourself as you can. Being angry at someone, or judgmental is not being nice to yourself. As you open your heart and fill up with loving yourself, you will look out at the world through loving eyes. And your love will spill out to other people with no strings attached.

Choices, Choices...

We have an experience when we say "I can't".

We have another experience when we say "I won't" or "I won't until my conditions are met".

We have still another experience when we say "I will".

Honesty is a Privilege

It's a privilege to be honest in this world that educates us to keep secrets.

I don't have to believe
everything I believe.

Some of my most original ideas, I got from other people.

In a worry or fear story, if something bad happens to you, you know you're turning your anger in.

Worry is a story I create about future events with a bad outcome.

Rules, Rules…

1. *Golden rule.*

2. *Platinum rule: Do unto yourself as you would have others do unto you.*

3. *Silver (library) rule: Do unto yourself what you would have others do unto themselves.*

4. *Rules are like pea pods. When the peas are ready, discard the pod.*

5.   *One of the unexpected perquisites of older age is the opportunity to free up your inhibited inner child from all those rules, rules, rules...*

BIBLIOGRAPHY

1. RAPKIN, M. Pretending, Thinking and Feeling in Psychotherapy, Voices, 1974, 10 (1), 14-21

2. RAPKIN, M. Discovering the Double Pretend Voices, 1975 (2) 70-73

3. RAPKIN, M. Anger as a Hot Potato - Constructive Options in Handling Anger, Voices, 1977, 13 (2) 66-74

4. RAPKIN, M., Is "Justified Anger" an Evasion of Reality An Essay on Addictive Anger, Dawnpoint. Association for Humanistic Psychology. Winter, 1978 17-21

www.ingramcontent.com/pod-product-compliance
Lightning Source LLC
Chambersburg PA
CBHW030424290526
45786CB00001B/122